Oversupply

Global mining to 2050

Martin Lynch

ISBN: 978-0-6488236-7-4 (paperback)

Published in Australia by Martin Lynch and InHouse Publishing.
www.inhousepublishing.com.au

Printed in Australia by InHouse Print & Design.

IN HOUSE PTY LTD PUBLISHING

NATIONAL LIBRARY OF AUSTRALIA

A catalogue record for this book is available from the National Library of Australia

Contents

Introduction

This book is about how the global mining industry is likely to develop over the next 30 years. It is the final instalment in a series of four books which deal with how global industrialisation shapes and drives the global mining industry.

Given its title, it is not giving too much away to say that the conclusion of this book is that the global mining industry is heading into a prolonged period of oversupply. This is mainly driven by the slowing of demand.

Whilst the declines forecast in this book are nearly unprecedented, prolonged periods of slow demand growth are standard fare in the history of global mining. Since the modern industrial world emerged in the 1870s global mining has shown a pattern of alternating periods of strong and weak growth. This is because it is driven by the global rate of urbanisation and industrialisation, which in its turn has shown itself to be prone to alternating periods of strong and weak growth.

To elaborate on this, since 1880 there have been three periods during which the world has experienced a high rate of urbanisation and industrialisation, and there have been two periods during which the rate has been much slower.

The sequence went like this:

- *Rapid growth from 1880 to 1930,* during which the nations of North America and Western Europe went from being predominantly agricultural economies with most people living on farms and in small to medium sized rural towns, to being urbanised economies with half their people living in cities. This process of urbanisation was made possible by the railway networks which came into being during the 1860s and 70s, the invention of new farm machinery, and the development of a new type of commercial organisation – large vertically integrated corporations – which emerged during the 1880s. The new corporations built much larger factories, and the railways allowed their mass-produced goods to be sent from their city-based factories to a wide geographical area. With the city-based factories replacing the town-based workshops, and with the new machines leading to mechanised farming, the displaced farm workers and workshop artisans packed up their families and belongings and moved to the cities.

- *Slow growth from 1930 to 1950,* as the Great Depression was followed by the Second World War in the nations of North America and Western Europe. During the Depression the rate of urbanisation and industrialisation not only slowed, it virtually came to a halt except in two newly-industrialising nations, Japan and Soviet Russia. There was a resurgence of activity once the war began but it was all devoted to the manufacture of armaments. The truly resource-intensive work of building, and re-building, cities did not resume until the war was over.
- *Rapid growth from 1950 to 1975,* during which the nations of North America and Western Europe went through a second stage of urbanisation. This time they were joined by Japan. The driving force behind this new stage of urbanisation was the desire of city dwellers to have larger houses. So they moved out of the urban centres and set-up on the fringes where there was more land. The locations they settled in were not really in the urban areas, but neither were they really in the rural areas. Someone coined the term "the sub-urban areas", which soon was shortened to the suburbs. Essentially the move to the suburbs involved rebuilding the cities. The motor vehicle was indispensable in allowing this to happen because in a suburban setting it was no longer the

case that all necessary shops were with walking distance. Cars required roads, and that led to entirely new, and much larger, transport networks being constructed.

- *Slow growth from 1975 to 2000,* which is the period following the end of the rush to the suburbs. By the time the mid 70s arrived the nations of North America, Western Europe, Japan and the Soviet Union, had reshaped their cities so that they now consisted of a city centre and concentric circles of inner-city suburbs and outer suburbs. The shift to the suburbs was not over, its just that it had slowed down to roughly match the rate of population growth. So the rate of urbanisation and industrialisation slowed down too.
- *Rapid growth from 2000 to 2015,* during which China followed in the path of the already-urbanised nations, moving from an agricultural economy to an urbanised and industrialised one.

These periods of rapid then slow growth in global industrialisation inevitably have flowed through to the global mining industry. For this reason, since 1880, there have been three periods of strong growth in global demand for minerals and metals, and two periods of slow growth. The next thirty years , as will be seen, will be the third period of slow growth.

This book is in two sections. The first looks at global demand over the next thirty years in four mineral sectors: copper ore, bauxite, iron ore and coal. A quantitative forecast is made for each sector to 2050. The second section looks at the global supply outlook for each of those same sectors. The overall picture which emerges is one of decades of significant over-supply. It is a gloomy outlook but one which will not last forever. The post-2050 period holds promise of a new period of very strong growth in demand..

Chapter 1

MINERAL DEMAND TO 2050

The Stages of Economic Growth

In forecasting global mineral demand for the next thirty years it is necessary to break the globe down into manageable pieces. The approach which will be taken here breaks the globe into seven different regions, and a forecast is made for each. The regions are:

- **Latin America**, which includes Mexico and all the countries to its south.
- **Sub-Saharan Africa**, which includes all the countries of the African continent except those which face onto the Mediterranean Sea.
- **South East Asia**, which includes all the countries of continental Asia which are south of China and east of India. It also includes the Philippines, Indonesia, Papua New Guinea and Timor Leste.
- **Kazakhstan-Morocco Crescent**, which includes all the countries of the MENA group (Middle East and North Africa) as well as Turkey, Pakistan and the Muslim-majority nations which were once part of the Soviet Union.

- The **Advanced Countries**, which includes the countries of North America, Europe as far east as Russia and the four Asian nations of Japan, Taiwan, South Korea and Singapore.
- **China**, which includes only China.
- **India**, which includes only India.

The case for taking this regional approach has been made, and hopefully well-established, in the third book in this series, *The Path of Industrialisation: 1880 to 2050.*[1]

Having chosen the seven global regions for which forecasts will be made, the next issue to determine is how to make these regional forecasts. The forecasts are built upon three assumptions:

1. Assumption 1. There are four stages of economic development which each country or region goes through on its journey from being a predominantly agricultural economy to being a post-industrial services-based economy. These stages are explained in *The Path of Industrialisation.*
2. Assumption 2. For the period 2020 to 2050, it is possible to forecast which of these four stages of economic development each of the seven global regions will be in. This forecast is made in *The Path of Industrialisation.*
3. Assumption 3. For each of the four stages of economic development there is a characteristic "intensity of use" of each of the mainstream metals and energy. This is a critical assumption and it is discussed in detail in the next section of this chapter.

Before broaching this subject, however, it is necessary to briefly recap the main points and conclusions from *The Path of Industrialisation.*

The main argument underpinning the book is that each country and region of the world follows the same sequence of developmental stages as it progresses from being an agricultural economy to being a post-industrial services-focussed economy. This notion was first systematically explored in a book, *The Stages of Economic Growth,*[2] written by the economist Walt Whitman Rostow and published in 1960. In the book he proposed a model which consists of a sequence of stages which nations pass through in their journey from being an agricultural to an urbanised "mass consumption" economy.

A similar model is used in *The Path of Industrialisation.* It goes like this: all countries prior to embarking on the path of industrialisation are in the **Agricultural stage**. When they commence their journey along the path, each country passes through two stages of industrial development. The first of these involves farm workers moving to the large towns and cities. During this period there is plenty of investment in city building and factory construction. This is called the **Urban stage**. The second stage of industrial development begins when the cities are established and the industrial base is in place. The economy then shifts to being focused on the building of a consumer society. Households are upgraded, made larger and are filled with all the latest consumer goods. This is called the **Household stage**. When this stage has run its course, as happened in the 1970s in the Advanced Countries, there is a third stage, which the Advanced Countries are now in. It is called the **Innovative Services stage**.

As has been said above, in *The Path of Industrialisation* a forecast was made of which stage of development each of the seven global regions will be in during the period 2020 to 2050:

- **Sub-Saharan Africa** will continue in the Agricultural stage over the next thirty years.
- **Latin America**, having languished in the Urban stage for decades now, will shift into the Household stage in the 2020s and continue moving through it for the next thirty years.
- The **Kazakhstan-Morocco Crescent**, unable to unify its fractured societies, will continue to languish in the Urban stage through to 2050.
- **South East Asia** will be a region of strong Urban stage economic growth through to 2050.
- **China** has completed its Urban stage development but will be stalled in that stage to 2050, unable to enact the needed social and economic reforms to allow it to progress to the Household stage.

- **India** will continue its strong progress through the Urban stage, completing it by the mid 2030s. At that point it will, like China, find that it cannot muster the political will to enact the needed reforms to allow it to shift into the Household stage. So it too will languish in the Urban stage to 2050.
- The **Advanced Countries** have now completed the Innovative Services stage and are stuck there, unable to break away from decades-old habits of tax cuts and deregulation which define that stage. The region will regain its political momentum when the productivity gains from robotics, and the urban rebuilding due to climate change, begin to really have an impact, probably by the late 2030s. At this point the region will enter an entirely new stage of development: the Robotic Services stage.

In the following chapters, this broad economic outlook will be translated into a forecast for global mineral and metal demand to 2050. The forecast will focus on the Big Four minerals and metals: steel, copper, aluminium and coal. These four are chosen because they are, and will remain for the next thirty years, the largest mineral and metal sectors. It is true that there are many other important mineral sectors, and some – especially those which are important in renewable energy production – will be fast-growing. Nevertheless, the focus will remain on this Big Four. To broaden the focus is to run the risk of an overly long book which provides more detail without shedding much more light.

Intensity of Use

It is now time to tackle the all-important issue of "intensity of use". The first thing to do is define what is meant by that term. The notion of the intensity of use of metals and materials will be familiar to most readers. There are two main ways in which it is commonly used. One is to gauge the quantity of metal or material used per $M of GDP. The other is to gauge the quantity of metal or material used per person. In this forecast, only the second measure will be used. Intensity of use in this book will, therefore, be defined as the weight of metal or mineral which is used each year in a region or country, divided by the number of people living in that region or country. It will be expressed in kilograms per person.

The assumption which underpins the forecasts made in this book is that for every country, or global region, at a given stage of economic development, the intensity of use of metal or energy is more or less the same regardless of *when* it passes through that stage.

This may come as a surprise to many readers, and the reality is in fact a bit more complicated than that. But it is fundamentally true. To provide an example: the intensity of use of copper in 1910s United States was about the same as the intensity of use of copper in 2010s China. In the 1910s the United States was coming to the end of its Urban stage development, likewise China was coming to the end of that stage during the 2010s. To generalise this: history has shown that, in each stage of economic development, there is a characteristic intensity of use of energy and mainstream metals

The statement "history has shown that, in each stage of economic development, there is a characteristic intensity of use" is not quite true. It is more accurate to say that there are in fact *two* characteristic intensities of use for each stage of economic development. Some regions at the same stage of economic development will have a far higher intensity of use than other regions. This is because, when a region embarks on the path of industrialisation and urbanisation, it does so either at High Speed or at Low Speed.

To illustrate what is meant by this, steel provides a good place to start. History shows that no matter what region of the world is considered, before that region embarks on the path to industrialisation, its intensity of steel use is typically in the range of 20 to 50 kilograms per person. When that region moves into the Urban stage of industrialisation, it will either be at High Speed or at Low Speed.

In the case of a High Speed transformation, a country's steel intensity quickly rises to 100kg, then it rises further to 200kg as the

Urban stage progresses. By the end of the Urban stage it is around 350kg per person or even higher. Then when this High Speed region enters the Household stage, its steel intensity of use goes even higher, up to 400 or 500kg per person. There have so far been two High Speed regions: the Advanced Countries and China.

Turning to the Low Speed regions, in these regions the rate of increase in the intensity of steel use is nowhere near as fast. By the end of the Urban stage, instead of being 350kg per person, in the Low Intensity regions the intensity of steel use is more like 100kg. The difference is clearly shown by comparing China's steel intensity of use at the end of its Urban stage to Latin America's at the same point. Latin America peaked at about 90kg per person back in 1975. China's peaked at 490kg in 2015.[3]

Whether a region falls into the High or Low Speed category can be determined by three factors:

1. *The speed at which GDP is growing.* Not every region progresses through each stage at the same pace. The faster the region is growing, the higher will be the intensity of use of all minerals and metals.
2. *The size of the manufacturing base which is being built.* Not all manufacturing bases are the same size relative to the overall economy. The larger it is, the higher the intensity.
3. *The rate at which high-rise residential accommodation is being built.* The more high-rise apartment buildings are in the urban accommodation mix, the higher will be the intensity.

The case of Latin America versus China can again be used to illustrate these differences. During their respective Urban stages, the rate of GDP growth was considerably slower in Latin America (4% per year) than in China (9% per year). As for the manufacturing base, the Latin American region constructed a much smaller manufacturing base than did China. And in Latin American the pattern of urban development involved far fewer high-rise apartment buildings than in China. All of which meant that Latin America had a very much lower intensity of steel use than did China.

Latin America is not the only region to follow this lower steel intensity path. The Kazakhstan-Morocco Crescent (excluding the Gulf States) has done the same, for similar reasons. India is also following that path. China, as already noted, is in the High Speed group, as was Japan and the other Advanced Countries. South-East Asia is a more mixed bag but, for the purposes of this forecast, has been included in the High Speed group. Sub-Saharan Africa has not yet embarked on the pathway to industrialisation, but when it eventually does it will certainly fall into the Low Speed group.

Having made these distinctions, it is necessary to put all this into numbers. Table 4.1 shows the intensity of use for steel, aluminium, copper and energy at different stages of economic development for the period 2020-50. As can be seen there are different intensities of use for the High Speed and Low Speed regions in the both the Urban and Household stages. No such distinction has been made in the Innovative Services stage because only one region, the Advanced Countries, has reached that stage.

Table 4.1: Intensity of use by stage of development.

		Agricultural	Urban		Household		Innovative services
			Low speed	High speed	Low speed	High speed	
Steel	kg/cap	40	100	300	120	550	400
Copper	kg/cap	1	2	6	2.5	8	9
Aluminium	kg/cap	1	4	10	8	30	40

The numbers in the table are derived from a variety of sources. Chief among them are:

- Annual Reports issued by the World Steel Association and its predecessor, the International Iron and Steel Institute.
- Occasional Special Reports issued by the United States Geological Survey (USGS).

Other sources have been reports by the International Copper Study Group and World Aluminium.

While the figures in the table are derived from actual historical statistics, they have, in some cases, been modified to reflect the expected changes over the next thirty years. These modifications are not made lightly, because there is quite a bit of stability over time in the intensity of use numbers.

The case of copper illustrates this stability over time. In the industrialising United States of the early 20th century, the intensity of copper use grew from 2kg per person in 1900 to 6kg in 1912, with an average of 4-5kg over that period.[4] In China between 1990 and 2010, the intensity of use of copper rose from about 2kg to 8kg, with an average of about 6kg. These numbers are very similar, surprisingly so given the fact that they are separated by 100 years.

The similarity reflects what will be called here the "Off-Set Law" of metal consumption. The Off-Set Law applied to copper goes like this: as the number of copper-containing products consumed per person goes up, so the quantity of copper required in each of those products goes down. There is no cause and effect relationship in this, it is just a manifestation of the general fact that as production of an item increases so too does the efficiency of production of that item. In the China of the first decade of the 21st century there were far more copper-containing items in common use than there were in the United States of the first decade of the 20th century. But it is also true to say that each of the items made in 2010 contained much less copper than those made in 1910.

All of this is meant to underline the point that caution must be exercised before making any forecast which incorporates a significant shift in intensity of use beyond the historical level. That said, there are times when new products come along which do result in such shifts occurring.

The electric vehicle, or EV, is one good example of such a new product. It will drive the intensity of use of copper above historical levels. The estimate made for this forecast is that it will increase the intensity of copper use in the Advanced Economies from 8 kilograms per person to 9 kilograms over person. Why this is expected to happen is discussed in some detail in the Box beginning on page 13.

As for the intensity of use of aluminium, it has been driven continually upwards over the past 100 years by a procession of new uses for the metal. To name just a few: aluminium kitchen utensils, electrical cables, aircraft bodies, window frames and vehicle engine bodies. The result has been that a country which is in the Urban stage today will have a far higher intensity of aluminium use than a country which was at the exact same stage 50 years ago. In aluminium's case, history is not repeating itself. It is being made anew each decade.

Having discussed how the intensity of use figures are derived, it is time to move to assigning specific intensities of use to specific regions. In order to do this, each region of the world must be assigned to one of the columns in Table 4.1. Table 4.2 shows how the regions have been assigned.

Table 4.2: Stage of development each region will be in between 2020 and 2050.

<table>
<tr><th rowspan="2"></th><th rowspan="2">Agricultural</th><th colspan="2">Urban</th><th colspan="2">Household</th><th rowspan="2">Innovative/ Robotic services</th></tr>
<tr><th>Low speed</th><th>High speed</th><th>Low speed</th><th>High speed</th></tr>
<tr><td>Advanced countries</td><td></td><td></td><td></td><td></td><td></td><td style="background:#bbb"></td></tr>
<tr><td>Latin America</td><td></td><td></td><td></td><td style="background:#bbb"></td><td></td><td></td></tr>
<tr><td>China</td><td></td><td></td><td style="background:#bbb"></td><td></td><td></td><td></td></tr>
<tr><td>South East Asia</td><td></td><td></td><td style="background:#bbb"></td><td></td><td></td><td></td></tr>
<tr><td>Kazakhstan to Morocco</td><td></td><td style="background:#bbb"></td><td></td><td></td><td></td><td></td></tr>
<tr><td>India</td><td></td><td style="background:#bbb"></td><td></td><td></td><td></td><td></td></tr>
<tr><td>Sub-Saharan Africa</td><td style="background:#bbb"></td><td></td><td></td><td></td><td></td><td></td></tr>
</table>

Five of these assignments will probably be seen as unremarkable. Two are more contentious. Probably the most contentious is India being regarded as a Low Speed industrialiser. After all, India has had nearly 20 years of rapid economic growth. Whilst this growth has not been as rapid as China's, it has at least been comparable with China. The country is sometimes even dubbed the "next China". Why, therefore, should India not be regarded as a High Speed industrialiser?

This is because just having a high rate of economic growth is not enough to qualify to be China's following act. India has only one of the three characteristics which make a High Speed industrialiser. That is, it has a high rate of GDP growth. The other two characteristics of a High Speed industrialiser are (1) a large manufacturing sector relative to its economy, and (2) a large proportion of the population moving into high-rise residential living quarters. India does not tick either of those boxes. It has a small manufacturing sector and a slow rate of urbanisation, and the majority of the people who are living in urban areas are not moving into high-rise apartment blocks. Which is why India falls into the Low Speed industrialiser group.

The other assignment which may be seen as contentious is characterising South East Asia as a region which will be going through the Urban stage at High Speed over the next 30 years. China is the classic High Speed industrialiser, as was Japan before it. The countries of South East Asia are at best pale imitations of China and Japan. Yet the region still ticks two of the three boxes to qualify as a High Speed industrialiser. It already has, and is still building, a large manufacturing sector relative to the size of its economy. And it has a high rate of GDP growth, near to, or even as high as, the Indian rate. It does not really tick the third box, because although the region has a high rate of urbanisation, its cities are still in the low-rise urban-sprawl mode of development. It is quite possible, however, that this will change in the next ten years and high-rise apartments buildings may well become the dominant type of newly constructed accommodation. Whatever happens in that respect, South East Asia, for the purposes of this forecast, is considered to be a High Speed industrialiser going through the Urban stage over the next 30 years.

Combining Tables 4.1 and 4.2, and factoring in the complexities discussed above, allows an estimate of intensities of use by region in 2030 and 2050. These are shown in Table 4.3. The base year is 2015.

Table 4.3: Intensities of use by region (2015, 2030 and 2050).

Region	Economic stage	Steel intensity of use			Copper intensity of use			Aluminium intensity of use		
		2015	2030	2050	2015	2030	2050	2015	2030	2050
Advanced countries	Innovative services	405	400	400	7.0	9.0	9.0	25.0	35.0	40.0
China	Urban – High speed	495	550	550	7.0	8.0	8.0	18.0	27.0	30.0
Latin America	Household – Low speed	130	130	130	1.2	2.5	2.5	4.0	8.0	8.0
Kazakhstan to Morocco	Urban – Low speed	100	120	120	1.2	5.2	2.5	4.0	8.0	8.0
South East Asia	Urban – High speed	143	200	400	1.2	4.0	8.0	4.0	6.6	13.3
India	Urban – Low speed	67	120	120	0.8	2.0	2.5	3.0	4.0	8.0
Sub-Saharan Africa	Agricultural	19	40	40	0.1	1.0	1.0	0.2	2.0	4.0

It is worthwhile taking a moment here to draw-out the most important assumptions made in this table.

Taking steel first, the key assumption is that China's steel intensity of use over the next 30 years will be 550kg per person. It will be recalled that, during the next 30 years, China is expected to be marooned in the transition zone between the Urban and Household stages. Table 4.1 says that the intensities of use of steel in the High Speed Urban and Household stages are 300 and 550kg respectively, meaning that a reasonable estimate for a country in the transition zone between those two stages would be about 425kg per person. For China to 2050, this has been increased to 550kg per person. This recognises the historical fact that the East Asian nations in the Advanced Countries region - Japan, South Korea and Taiwan – have all had much higher intensities of steel use than the rest of the nations in that region (about 800 kg/person versus about 500 kg/person). China is following much the same path as Japan, and as result it is expected to have a higher intensity of use than would other countries at the same stage. Hence the forecast of 550kg rather than 425. It must be said that this is, as they say, a big call. Because the forecast for China's steel intensity (will it be 425kg or 550kg, or maybe even 625kg?) has a very important influence on the overall forecast for global steel consumption over the next thirty years.

Turning to aluminium, the key assumption is that the intensity of use in the Advanced Countries and China will keep on climbing over the forecast period. As of 2015 it was 25kg per person in the Advanced Countries and 18kg in China. The forecast is that by 2050 it will be 40kg and 30kg respectively. This rather bullish prediction is dependent on a further critical assumption: that the demand for aluminium is to a large extent independent of the rate of growth of the economy as a whole. This has been true in the Advanced Economies for decades. Intensity of use has grown from 16kg per person in 1990 to nearly 30kg in 2020 despite the sluggish economic growth rates over that time.

As for copper, the key assumption is that the intensity of use in the Advanced Countries will rise at a modest rate, as it will in China. In other words, the demand for copper will not take-off, despite the restructuring in the next 30 years of the most of the world's power production and distribution networks.

Having established estimates of intensity of use for steel, copper and aluminium by region over the next thirty years, it is a straightforward matter to calculate how much global demand should grow between now and 2050. All that is needed is an estimate of how regional populations will increase over that period, and such estimates are readily available from a range of sources. The estimates used in this forecast come from the United Nations Department of Economic and Social Affairs.

The resultant forecast for global demand for copper, aluminium and steel is shown in Table 4.4. The alert reader will notice that coal consumption has not so far been discussed, nor is there a forecast for it in Table 4.4. This is because coal use has to be considered within the context of the overall energy mix, and the global energy mix will in the next thirty years undergo changes which have no historical precedent. For this reason, coal is considered in a separate chapter later in this section.

Table 4.4: Global metal consumption: actual and forecast.

		2015	2030	2050
Copper	Mt/a	23	36	43
Aluminium	Mt/a	72	114	149
Steel	Mt/a	1616	1937	2190

It can be seen from the table that global copper demand is expected to double between 2015 and 2050, and aluminium is expected to go up even more. Steel is the slow mover, increasing by only about 40%. Looked at on a global per capita basis, the intensity of use of copper and aluminium will rise substantially from current levels, but it will stay about steady for steel.

These forecasts look at total global metal demand. A forecast for total metal demand is one thing. A forecast for mined metal demand is a different thing. In order to make that forecast, it is necessary to estimate the role which will be played by recycled metal. This is considered in the next chapter.

The Electric Vehicle

Mechanised transport began with the steam locomotive, and that machine reigned unchallenged from the 1810s to the 1880s. The 1890s brought two new engines into the mainstream of commercial life: the electric motor and the internal combustion engine. With their arrival, it did not take long before the steam-driven locomotive had some competition.

For a while these three engines competed with each other for supremacy in the newly-invented automobile. In 1900, there were some 4,200 automobiles manufactured in the United States. Of those, about 1,700 were steam powered, 1,600 were battery powered and 900 were powered by the internal combustion engine.[5]

As the motor for an automobile, each of the three engines had something to recommend it. The steam engine had familiarity, the electric motor had superior performance and the internal combustion engine had ease of use. In the race for customer acceptance, the internal combustion engine had gained the lead by 1905, and had effectively won the day by 1910. By then Henry Ford had been producing Model T's for two years and they used the internal combustion engine. By 1915, the great majority of automobiles were doing the same.

The main advantage of the internal combustion engine lay in the fuel it used. Petrol is a very concentrated form of energy, so an automobile could store enough of it to travel quite long distances before having to refuel. And when refuelling was eventually necessary, petrol was easy to find. Most road-side retail outlets kept bottles of it for sale. This contrasted with the electric car, which could travel only short distances before the battery needed recharging. When it did need recharging, charging stations were few and far between. It also contrasted with the steam engine. Petrol is a much more concentrated form of energy than wood or charcoal. In contrast to the petrol-driven car, the steam-driven car had to stop much more often for re-fuelling, and was also a much more maintenance-intensive engine.

Having won the day by 1915, for the last one hundred years the internal combustion engine has been largely unchallenged in road transport applications. Its performance improvements have left the steam engine far behind. But the electric motor has kept pace with it. In fact, as an automobile engine, the electric motor still rivals, and even outperforms, the internal combustion engine.

The trouble with the electrically-powered vehicle has always been its fuel-carrying capability. It has been difficult to find a battery capable of storing enough electricity on-board the vehicle without greatly overloading it.

Things are changing. These days the ability to store electricity on-board an automobile is improving rapidly. The lithium-ion battery is the latest in a long line of improved batteries. It is the best so far in its electricity storage density, which is the measure of how much energy can be stored per weight or volume of battery. In other words, the lithium ion battery can store more useable electricity than any other battery for a given size and weight of that battery.

Such is its advantage over previous batteries that the lithium ion battery is now used in mass-market electric vehicles. Of them, the Tesla is the best-known, but the Tesla most certainly does not have the market to itself. In fact, the electric vehicle market is becoming crowded. By the mid 2020s, it is likely that all the existing internal combustion vehicle manufacturers, and a bunch of new electric vehicle-only manufacturers, will be offering their own models. In the next ten years, the electric vehicle is expected to become a commonplace automobile instead of the novelty that it is today.

The shift to the electric vehicle is one of those technical advances – which are few and far between – which has the potential to greatly change the intensity of use of one or more metals. It will have a big impact on the intensity of use of lithium, manganese, cobalt and nickel, because these are the metals which make-up the most commonly used lithium battery for automobiles. It will also have an impact on the intensity of use of copper.

Why copper? A standard internal combustion engine-powered automobile contains about 25 kilograms of copper. About half of it is used in the wiring harness, which is the complex web of wiring which transmits electrical power through the vehicle and connects the vehicle's sensors and actuators to on-board computers. The rest of it is used in motor windings, battery cables, switches, sensors and also in the engine and chassis. A standard electric motor-driven automobile needs another 55 kilograms or so of copper. This is almost all used as windings in the stator of the electric motor.

To explain this: most electric cars use what is known as a squirrel cage induction motor. This consists of a stator and a rotor. The stator is a stationary hollow cylinder. Sitting inside the stator is a rotatable core known as the rotor. The whole thing works when the windings on the stator are energised by electric current coming from the battery. This creates a rotating magnetic field in the stator and, through the magic of electromagnetic interaction, that sets the rotor spinning. The rotor's rotational energy is then transferred to the vehicle's drive shaft, thereby propelling the vehicle into motion.

Having described where the extra copper will be used in the electric vehicle, how much additional annual global copper consumption is it realistic to expect from it?

To begin to get a handle on this, the total number of cars and trucks manufactured each year across the globe is now about 120 million.[6] The great majority of these new vehicles are powered by internal combustion engines. Using the figure of 25 kilograms of copper per car, the copper contained in last year's newly manufactured vehicles was about three million tonnes. If all of those vehicles were electric vehicles made using a copper rotor, then that same total of 120 million new vehicles would have consumed about nine million tonnes of copper. So if every new vehicle was manufactured with a battery-powered squirrel cage motor, rather than an internal combustion engine, current global copper demand would increase by about one third.

But this is a theoretical outcome only. To get a realistic sense of how much additional copper demand will come from the electric vehicle in, say, 2040, three factors must be estimated: how many vehicles of any kind will be manufactured in 2040? How many of those will use the squirrel cage induction motor, versus using the internal combustion engine or the fuel cell motor? And how many of the induction motors will use copper in the rotor and stator as opposed to aluminium, which is often used in other squirrel cage motor applications?

To estimate the total number of vehicles likely to be manufactured in 2040, three main assumptions can be made: the total number of new vehicles purchased in the Developed Economies will not change much from the current level, in China it is likely to double between 2020 and 2040 and in the rest of the world it could increase by half from current levels. Taken together, this means that total new vehicle manufacture in 2040 will increase by about 50% from current levels, meaning that 180 million vehicles will be manufactured in that year.

Of these, it is quite probable that a high proportion will be electric vehicles. A reasonable estimate seems to be that 75% of new vehicles will be electric or at least full hybrid.

Of these vehicles many will be going to lower income countries, and to lower income consumers within the Advanced Countries. This fact, along with the likelihood that the price of copper will be higher than it is today, suggests that a good proportion of the induction motors used in new vehicles will be using aluminium in the motor instead of copper.[7] A reasonable estimate seems to be that two in five vehicles will use aluminium, and that may well be an underestimate.

Doing the maths using these estimates, by 2040 global copper demand would be higher by about four million tonnes per year thanks to electric vehicles. Given that global consumption is set to rise in the vicinity of twenty million tonnes per year (including the contribution from electric vehicles), the rise of the electric vehicle is indeed set to drive up the intensity of use of copper but it will not revolutionise the market.

Urban Mining

The recycling of metals is familiar to everyone. Fewer people, however, would know just how important is the contribution of recycled metal to global metal markets. In part this is because it is rarely spoken about. The purpose of this section is to discuss how much more important recycled metal may become in the next thirty years.

It will help to start by getting some definitions clear. There are two types of recycled metal. One is factory scrap. These are metal off-cuts which are discarded in the process of manufacturing a commercial product. These off-cuts are sent back to the smelting plant and are melted down again. They never make their way into the world of real products.

The second type of recycled metal is old scrap. It is the only type which is of interest in this forecast. Old scrap comes from products that have been in commercial use, often for many years, and then are removed from that use due to obsolescence. Demolished buildings and unwanted equipment are the two most common sources.

Old scrap has always been a big contributor to the total tonnage of metal consumed around the world in any year. In 2015 it is estimated that nearly three out of every ten tonnes of steel used in the world was sourced from old scrap. In aluminium, old scrap was estimated to be responsible for one fifth of the metal consumed globally. In copper, old scrap made about the same contribution as in aluminium.

That is a big contribution. The old scrap steel recycled in 2015 was equivalent in tonnage to the steel which was smelted from all the iron ore produced in Brazil and India. In copper, the tonnage of old scrap which made its way into new products was the equivalent of the copper smelted from all the mines of the Copperbelt and China put together.

Because most of this old scrap comes from urban areas, it could be said that the cities of the world are steel, copper and aluminium mines. Hence the term urban mining. Clearly these urban mines are already big contributors to the total global supply. In the next thirty years, they will become even bigger contributors.

To begin considering this, the most useful place to start is by looking at the dynamics of scrap generation. All products have an average life expectancy. For example, a metal container used for storing food or drink has an expected life of about two months. An automobile has an expected life of about fifteen years. For a suburban house, the expected life is about forty years. A bridge or railway has a life expectancy of around one hundred years.

It is possible to calculate an average expected Time-in-Use for a metal if it is known approximately what percentage of the metal goes into each category of products. These surveys are regularly done, so that information is well known. It turns out that steel has an average Time-in-Use of about 28 years. Copper is not far behind. Its average Time-in-Use is about 25 years. As for aluminium, it is 20 years.[8]

It is worth dwelling on this for a moment. Aluminium has a Time-in-Use of 20 years versus steel's 28 years. Intuition would suggest that this is not quite right: should not aluminium have a far shorter average Time-in-Use than steel? After all, plenty of steel goes into bridges, tunnels and ports, all of which are designed for very long lives. Steel also goes into tall buildings which are intended to last many decades. In contrast, a lot of aluminium is used in packaging which does not even last six months.

What the intuition misses is that plenty of aluminium is also used in buildings, not as structural support but as door and window frames, trimming and cable racking. A good amount is also used in infrastructure such as long-distance electrical cables, and in aircraft which are usually in service for many decades.

If the average Time-in-Use estimates quoted above are accepted then it is straightforward enough to estimate how much scrap will be generated in any particular year. All that is needed is a knowledge of how much of the metal was installed 28 years ago (in the case of steel) or 20 years ago (in the case of aluminium).

That is a good start, but having an estimate of the quantity of old scrap generated in any year is not enough. It is also necessary to have a good estimate of how much of that old scrap will actually be brought back into use. This is known as the End-of-Life Recycle Rate. Like the average Time-in-Use, this varies for different metals. It also varies for different regions and countries.

Many estimates have been made of End-of-Life Recycle Rates. Globally, a commonly used estimate for steel's End-of-Life Recycle Rate is 60 to 70%.[9] This is quite a high rate. The reason why it is so high is that the easiest way to dispose of old automobiles, heavy pieces of machinery or the steel beams used in tall buildings is to take them to a scrap merchant. Not all steel is so easy to recycle. The steel product with the lowest End-of-Life Recycle Rate is rebar. It often ends up in landfill because it is too costly to separate from the cement in which it is encased.

For aluminium, the End-of-Life Recycle Rate is highly variable between product categories. The recycling of aluminium cans is impressively high, near 90%.[10] For other packaging – such as foil and wrapping – it is very low. For aluminium contained in large, easily-identifiable items, such as obsolete aircraft and overhead cables, the recycle rate is very high. As for the aluminium from demolished buildings, the rate is dependent on whoever is doing the demolition. Overall, the End-of-Life recycle rate for aluminium is estimated to be similar to steel: between 60 and 70%.

For copper, the global End-of-Life Recycle Rate is the lowest of the three. It is usually estimated at between 40 and 50%,[11] although more recent estimates suggest the rate is creeping up. Copper recycle is lower than steel or aluminium because a good deal of obsolete copper is quite difficult to recover. When it is in large motor windings or some other easily accessible form, the rate is high. However, if it is in household appliances it takes a lot of effort to break the appliance apart and get to the small copper-rich devices and then separate them out. Buildings present the same challenge: the copper in plumbing and wiring is spread throughout the structure and buried behind walls. It is often the case that recovering it for recycle is deemed not worth the time it would take. As a result, much of the copper contained in demolished buildings ends up in landfill. There it lies alongside the discarded copper-containing household appliances.

There are two factors which will influence how much the contribution of urban mining to future global metal consumption will increase. The first of these is whether the End-of-Life Recycle Rate will increase or stay about the same as the years go on. The second is how rapidly global demand for metal will grow in the next thirty years versus the previous thirty years.

Turning first to the End-of-Life Recycle Rates, they will almost certainly rise for steel and copper. It will rise for steel because the CO_2 emissions associated with smelting pig iron will make blast furnace-derived steel increasingly expensive. There may even legislative requirements imposed to limit the extent of such carbon-intensive steel manufacture. As for copper, the benchmark prices are likely to head in the upward direction over the next ten years at least, which will make it more worthwhile to recycle. Even if prices flatten out later on, or fall, the improvements in the process of copper recycle will be permanent.

As for the recycle rate for aluminium, the outlook is less certain. Electricity generated by renewable energy will probably be very cheap in a few decades from now and that will make aluminium very cheap. Which would lower the incentive to recycle scrap. For this reason, it is likely that the recycle rate will stay about the same for aluminium.

Table 4.5 shows the estimates for End-of-Life Recycle Rates for copper, steel and aluminium in the base year of 2015, and for 2030 and 2050.

Table 4.5: End-of-life recycle rates.

	2015	**2030**	**2050**
Steel	62%	68%	75%
Aluminium	65%	68%	70%
Copper	45%	55%	60%

The other factor which will determine the influence of urban mining on future metal consumption is the rate of growth in overall metal demand. To explain what is meant by this, take the hypothetical case of a metal with a 25-year average Time-in-Use. If the demand for this metal grows at 5% per year, by the end of year 25, the quantity of metal being used in year 25 will be 3.4 times higher than in year 1. In year 25, the metal used in year 1 will be coming out of use and (potentially at least) back onto the market. Which means that the metal available for recycle will be 30% of the total demand. If it is further assumed that the End-of-Life Recycle Rate is 50%, then the proportion of recycled metal in the total metal consumption for that year is 15%.

Using the same set of assumptions, but changing the growth rate to just 2% per year, the year 25 demand is only 1.6 times that of year 1. The contribution of recycled metal to the total metal consumption increases to 30%. In other words, the slower the growth rate in global metal demand over a long period of time, the higher is the contribution of recycled metal to the overall global production.

Experience bears this out. The years between 1970 and 1990 were slow demand growth years for global steel. As a result, nearly four out of ten tonnes of steel produced were being sourced from old scrap by the end of that period. In contrast, between 1995 and 2015, global demand for steel grew at a very fast rate. As a result, only three out of ten tonnes were being sourced from old scrap by the end of that period. To put it more succinctly: the slower the demand growth is for a metal over a certain period, the higher will be the percentage of it which is sourced from old scrap at the end of the period.

The contribution of recycled metal to total consumption is straightforward to calculate once the Time-in-Use, End-of-Life recycle rate and total consumption is known, or forecast, for any particular year. All these parameters are known for 2015, and forecast for 2030 and 2050. The table shows the forecast of the contribution of recycled metal to total global consumption in each of those years.

Table 4.6: Contribution of recycled metal to total global consumption.

	2015	2030	2050
Steel	28%	29%	58%
Aluminium	21%	18%	44%
Copper	21%	26%	41%

The numbers in the table clearly show that urban mining will be a much more important factor in global metal production in 2050 than it is today. Nearly 60% of steel consumed in that year will come from recycled steel. And more than two tonnes in every five of aluminium and copper consumed in 2050 will have been recycled. Which means that the contribution of metal smelted from newly-mined ore will fall rather sharply between 2020 and 2050. Before putting this all together into a full forecast for annual mined metal production in 2050, it is time to consider the thorny issue of the outlook for coal.

Coal in the Energy Mix

A good place to start the discussion about the future for coal is with a brief review of the current global distribution of energy consumption. This is shown in Table 4.7. The table also shows intensity of use for each region.

Table 4.7: Total energy use, and intensity of use, by region (2015).[12]

	Total use	Intensity of use
	MTOE	kg per capita
Advanced countries	6259	4542
China	2994	2221
Latin America	845	1083
South East Asia	738	717
Kazakhstan-Morocco	838	626
India	837	485
Sub-Saharan Africa	700	320
World	13,211	1790

Note that because of the many different types of energy, a way of directly comparing and adding them together is needed. To allow this to happen, each form of energy is expressed in terms of equivalent tonnes of oil. For example, a tonne of coal is expressed in terms of a tonne of Oil Equivalent. The total energy used is expressed in millions of tonnes of Oil Equivalent, or MTOE. The intensity of energy use is expressed as kilograms of Oil Equivalent per person.

It will be seen from the table that the Advanced Countries are currently accounting for nearly half of the world's total energy consumption, and China is responsible for nearly another quarter. Together they account for close to 70% of global energy use.

The reason that the Advanced Countries account for so much of the world's energy use is that in these countries the great majority of people have near universal access to all the modern conveniences: mechanised transport, air-conditioning and refrigeration in the home and at work, communications and the list goes on. China, despite its great progress over the last forty years, is still far behind the Advanced Countries in energy use per person, and most of its energy is used in industry. Its residential energy use remains far below that of the Advanced Countries. The rest of the world's regions are well behind even China. In India, the average person uses only one tenth of the energy consumed by the average person in the Advanced Countries. This highlights the fact that energy use is highly dependent on the stage of economic development. Table 4.8 shows the average intensity of energy use at each stage of economic development, broken into High and Low Speed industrialisers.

Table 4.8: Intensity of energy use by stage of development.

		Agricultural	**Urban**		**Household**		**Innovative services**
			Low speed	**High speed**	**Low speed**	**High speed**	
Energy	kg oil eq/cap	300	800	1500	1500	3200	4500

The numbers in Table 4.8 seem to indicate that there are big jumps in intensity of energy use between the end of one economic stage and the beginning of the next. This is not what happens. What actually happens is that energy intensity in all economies, be they Low or High Speed industrialisers, rises steadily from about the mid-point of the Urban stage right through to the end of the Household stage. In the Low Speed industrialisers the rise is considerably slower than in the High Speed industrialisers, but in both there is a rising trend. Once an economy reaches the end of the Household stage the energy intensity does not rise much further. In fact, the last 20 years in the Advanced Countries has seen energy intensity plateau. More recently it has begun to fall.

Coal is just one of the ingredients in the global energy mix. To consider what might happen with coal over the next thirty years, it will help to begin by looking at how it currently fits into the overall energy mix. Looking at the world as whole in 2018, coal provided a bit more than one quarter of the energy used. Petroleum and natural gas contributed over half. Taken together, the carbon-based fuels, which also include firewood, ethanol and other biomass sources, supplied 85% of the world's energy. Three quarters of the rest was supplied by two other traditional sources: hydro and nuclear power. The last little bit, about 4% of the world's energy, was supplied by the renewable energy sources of wind and solar.

Coal's contribution varied greatly by region. In two of them – hydropower-rich Latin America and the oil and gas-rich Kazakhstan-Morocco Crescent – it played a very small part. In two others – China and India – it supplied well over half of the energy used. In Sub-Saharan Africa, coal supplied about 15% of the energy mix, and in South East Asia the figure was about 20%. In the Advanced Countries, it was also about 20%.

Because both Sub-Saharan Africa and South East Asia are relatively small energy-consuming regions, the great majority of global coal consumption in 2018 occurred in just three of the global regions – China, India and the Advanced Countries. Together they accounted for more than 90%. Given this, when looking at how global coal consumption may change between 2020 and 2050, these three regions are really the only one's that matter.

As for the end uses of coal, there are really only two. One is in electricity generation and the other is in the provision of heating in industrial processes. In the Advanced Countries nearly all of the coal used is in electricity generation, with the remainder used as a source of heat in industrial processes such as cement making and chemical manufacture. In India, and especially in China, much more of the coal consumed is used directly as a fuel in industry. This is mainly for providing heat but in some cases, such as in steel making, the coal is also used as a structural input to the process. For each of the three regions, the proportion of coal used in electricity generation and industrial applications is shown in Table 4.9.

Table 4.9: Coal consumption by end-use sector.[13]

	Advanced countries	**China**	**India**	**Three regions**
Electricity generation	91	54	64	67
Direct in industry	9	46	36	33

To forecast the global demand for coal in 2050, it is best to consider separately the two, largely unrelated, issues of (1) coal's share of global electricity generation and (2) coal's share of the energy used in industrial heating. Of course, it is not enough just to forecast coal's share of these two activities, it is also necessary to forecast the total amount of energy which will be used in each. The following sections present in summary form the conclusions arrived at for the purposes of this forecast.

It is important point out that the forecast made here assumes that global energy use up to the 2040s will be governed for the most part by traditional economics. In other words there will be a reluctance on the part of most governments to cut CO_2 emissions if doing so creates serious, short-term economic losses. A forecast which takes a similar approach is the International Energy Outlook 2019, produced by the United States Energy Information Administration (EIA). It is worth noting that the forecast made here is similar to that arrived at in the EIA report.

Share of coal in electricity generation

In the **Advanced Countries**, the region's per capita use of electricity is expected to increase by 20% to 2050, in large part because of the widespread adoption of electric vehicles. As for coal's share of electricity generation, it will fall because the generation of electricity will shift further towards renewables and natural gas. Coal-fired power stations will be closed, particularly those that were built during the 1950s through to the 70s, such that by 2050 coal is forecast to produce only about 10% of the electricity used in the region, down from about 25% in 2020. In terms of tonnage, the amount of coal used in the region's electricity generation in 2050 will be half of what it was in 2020.

In **China**, the per capita use of electricity is forecast to increase by about 50% between 2020 and 2050, a much slower increase than in the previous 30 year period. About two thirds of this new capacity will come from wind and solar facilities, and much of the rest will come from new gas-fired and nuclear power stations. As for China's existing coal-based generation capacity, there will be a reluctance to close large parts of it because much of it is still relatively new. There will be closures of the old coal-fired capacity and that may well be replaced by modern coal-fired capacity. The overall result will be that coal will supply about half of the country's electrical power in 2050, down from about two thirds in 2020. The total tonnage of coal used in China's electricity generation will be about the same in 2050 as it was in 2020.

In **India**, the per capita use of electricity in 2050 is expected to have nearly tripled from its 2020 level as the country goes through the second half of its Urban stage of development and its population grows by one third. Much of this new capacity will come from coal-fired power stations but even more of it will come from renewables, which will be cheaper but will also have the disadvantages of being intermittent sources and needing much more land. By 2050, coal-fired power generation stations will be supplying nearly half of the nation's electricity, down from close to three quarters in 2020. In tonnage terms, the coal being used in electricity generation in 2050 is forecast to have nearly doubled from current levels.

The greatest uncertainty is the outlook for China. For a start, the forecast made here is completely out of step with what is required if China is to achieve its recently legislated target of zero greenhouse gas emissions by 2060. Yet even the forecast made here seems a tough target. For China to supply two thirds of its new electricity generation capacity from renewable energy plants is undoubtedly a tall order. Especially when a still-massive national resource of coal lies beneath the surface and the country is now the world leader in building large and very efficient coal-fired plants. China, it has to be emphasised, has long passed the point where it hastily constructs dirty coal-fired power plants just to generate cheap electricity. Supercritical (high efficiency, low emissions) coal-fired generators account for nearly half of the country's coal-fired capacity these days,[14] whereas they are relatively uncommon in the Advanced Countries which built its electricity production system between the 1950s and 1990s. As for the ultra-supercritical (very high efficiency) power plants, China has by far the largest number of any country in the world. Indeed, China has the world's most technically advanced coal-fired power generation network.

Yet even to achieve the forecast made here (let alone the net zero by 2060 target) it has to be assumed that China will turn away from its readily available coal and its considerable technical expertise in building high performance coal-fired generators, and will from now on concentrate on building renewable energy plants and, to a lesser extent, gas-fired power plants. Hard as that may be to believe, the signs are there that this is happening, and will continue to happen.

China is, after all, a country which has become accustomed to meeting new industrial and infrastructure challenges. Shifting in a big way into renewable energy, all the while retiring dirty coal plants and replacing them with cleaner, more efficient ones, is no more difficult than everything else the country has achieved since the 1980s.

Share of coal in industrial applications

As for the use of coal in industrial applications, the main assumptions are that by 2050:

- In the **Advanced Countries**, the coal used in steel, cement and other furnace-based processes will have fallen to almost nothing. This will be achieved by replacing the coal with a combination of natural gas and electricity. In the case of blast furnace steel making, to the extent that any such plants remain in operation they will be using hydrogen in place of pulverised coal.
- In **China**, a similar process of substitution will have taken place but the reduction of coal intensity in manufacturing is partly off-set by the fact that the manufacturing base is still growing. The tonnage of coal used in industrial applications in 2050 is expected to be about half of what it is in 2020.
- In **India**, the process of substituting coal with electricity or natural gas is expected to be much slower than in China, partly because of the lack of availability of gas. Also, the growth of the manufacturing base will be faster than in China. The forecast outcome is that total coal use in industrial applications is expected to be about 30% higher in 2050 than 2020.

Based on these assumptions, the tonnage of coal used directly in industrial applications across the world is expected to fall by 40% while the total energy used in those applications is expected to rise by at least one third. Coal will be substituted by electricity and natural gas.

The results of the forecast are shown in Table 4.10. Note that the coal consumption and intensity of use figures shown in the table are expressed in terms of actual tonnes of coal, not tonnes of oil equivalent. The forecast shows that the tonnage of coal used globally is expected to fall by nearly 20% between 2020 and 2050. Coal use in the Advanced Countries in 2050 is expected to be only about one quarter of its 2020 level, China is expected to stay steady and in India total coal use will have increased by about two thirds. Should China achieve its net zero emissions target by 2060, its coal consumption by 2050 will have to be well below the forecast 3.4 billion tonnes per annum. It would be at most 2 billion tonnes, most of which would come from the power generation network. Global coal consumption in 2050, instead of being about 20% less than 2020, would be one third down on 2020.

Table 4.10: Coal consumption by region: actual 2018 and forecast 2050.[15]

	Total coal consumption (Mt)	
	2018	**2050**
Developed	2246	597
China	3770	3433
India	982	1576
SS Africa	204	203
South East Asia	317	372
Kazakhstan-Morocco	40	35
Latin America	67	58
World	**7626**	**6274**

Before moving on from this subject, it is worthwhile making some observations on the matter of operating a stable national grid when more wind and solar power is being added. It sometimes said that the grid will become unstable if the proportion of intermittent sources, like wind and solar, takes too large a share of the electricity generation mix. This is an important issue to deal with because the assumptions made in the forecast envisage wind and solar providing, by 2050, about 40% of the national electrical power supply in the Advanced Countries and China.

It is assumed in this forecast that 40% renewables can be managed while maintaining a stable national grid. One of the reasons for making this assumption is that current experience is already coming close to this. Germany, a major industrial power with a population of some 83 million people, already has one third of its electrical power produced by wind and solar, and this with only a small capacity of energy storage to help smooth out the mismatch between demand and production. A second reason for making this assumption is that there is a consensus in the field that intermittent sources can rise to about 50% of the total without creating unmanageable instability.

In any case, should large-scale and widespread energy storage be needed to maintain grid stability, the technical options are quickly developing. Pumped storage, whereby water is pumped to an upper reservoir and then run through power-generating turbines en route to a lower reservoir, has long been an option. The first pumped storage plant was built in the 1920s, and the largest energy storage facility in the world today is a pumped storage plant in the US state of Virginia. Another option, similar to pumped storage, is stored compressed air, of which the largest plant is in Germany. A third option is the battery, and here a range of technologies are in use. The largest battery storage plant in world is in the Chinese province of Liaoning. It uses a vanadium-based technology. Another large battery storage facility is in Dubai, it uses sodium-sulphur technology first developed by the Ford Motor Company in the 1960s for use in automobiles. The largest lithium-ion battery storage plant is in the Australian state of South Australia,[16] and it is currently being increased in capacity by 50%.

With these existing energy storage options, and others which will no doubt emerge, the technical challenges of grid management which arise from the increasing use of intermittent power sources look to be in the process of being solved. Nevertheless, it is no small matter to shift a large national electricity grid away from coal when it is the dominant power-generating fuel. It is also no small matter to requisition the land needed for wind and solar plants. These are the challenges facing both China and India.

The forecast assumes that both countries will successfully deal with these challenges and greatly reduce their reliance on coal over the next thirty years. But to properly deal with global warming there needs to be a more rapid transition away from coal. This transition will begin gather pace when the fact of global warming can no longer be ignored – probably in the 2040s. At that point the reduction of coal use will take on a greater urgency.

Coal-fired power generation will, except for some isolated outposts, be a thing of the past by the 2080s.

Mineral Demand in 2050

It is time now to quantify the forecast for global consumption of steel, copper, aluminium and coal to 2050. This will include a forecast for the intermediate year, 2030.

The forecast has a central case. The main elements:

- The Chinese economy will, over the next thirty years, be far weaker as an engine of growth than it was during the past thirty. This is driven, in the main, by demographic decline and an increasingly repressive central government. This is the most important assumption underpinning this forecast because the Chinese economy has carried the global economy for the last two decades.
- The Indian economy will continue with its strong growth for another fifteen years or so, then will slow down as its main engine – the export of business services – loses its potency due to competition from artificial intelligence.
- The Advanced Countries will remain in the economic slow lane for the next twenty years as their governments keep on trying to recapture the glory days of the 1980s when tax cuts, union-busting and deregulation were new and exciting drivers of growth in the economy. This forecast contends that real economic growth will return in the late 2030s when new leaders emerge with fresh policies to harness the opportunities inherent in the issues of artificial intelligence, climate change and the aging of the population.

- Three of the other four regions of the world – Latin America, Kazakhstan-Morocco Crescent and Sub-Saharan Africa - will contribute little in the way of economic growth over the next thirty years, being stuck in social and political quagmires of longstanding.
- South East Asia will be the one region of the world where economic growth rates are above the historical average, mostly due to the emergence of the so-called Late Starter group of Vietnam, Myanmar, Bangladesh and Cambodia.
- There will be a steadily growing level of action to mitigate climate change and this will shift all countries towards renewable energy and away from coal. But this will only become a sharp, rather than a steady, shift when the impact of climate change really becomes apparent during the 2040s.
- The recycling of metals will become a major force in global metal markets from the 2030s as China's cities start a rebuilding phase.

It goes without saying that there are uncertainties in all this. The biggest uncertainty relates to China. That country's economic performance over the next 30 years will have a very strong influence on the forecast. Should China's economy continue at somewhere near its rate of the past twenty years, then this forecast will go the way of many others: in other words, it will be very wide of the mark.

Another important uncertainty is the world's response to global warming. This forecast sees it having little influence until the mid 2040s. However the response could be much more robust and could conceivably drive demand for metals to new heights if world-wide urban restructuring in order to counter worsening weather begins in the 2030s. At the same time this more robust response would drive coal consumption much lower than forecast.

Having established these general propositions and uncertainties, the base case forecast for metal and coal consumption to 2050 is shown in the Table 4.11. The table also shows the forecast for 2030. This intermediate year is included because consumption growth rates in the period 2030 to 2050 are quite different to the period 2015 to 2030.

Table 4.11: Forecast for global metal and coal consumption.

		2015	2030	2050	Annual inc 2015-30	Annual inc 2030-50	2050 % of 2015
Copper	Mt/a	23	36	43	3.0%	1.0%	188%
Aluminium	Mt/a	72	114	149	3.1%	1.3%	208%
Steel	Mt/a	1616	1937	2190	1.3%	0.6%	136%
Coal	Mt/a	7592	7423	6252	-0.1%	-0.8%	82%

Looking first at the period 2015 to 2030, the annual growth in demand for copper and aluminium is fairly strong, at somewhere near the average of the last hundred years. This is because both the Advanced Countries and China are still increasing in their intensity of use of both metals, not rapidly but steadily. Steel, however, shows weak growth, considerably slower than the average of the past hundred years. This is because China's recent decades of breakneck consumption growth will not continue, so there is no longer an engine of steel demand in the global market large enough to off-set the virtually zero growth which has long been the case in the Advanced Countries. As for coal, the only engine of any size driving coal demand is India and this is being off-set by a steep reduction of coal consumption in the Advanced Countries. Coal's annual rate of demand growth over the 15 years from 2015 to 2030 is slightly less than zero.

This somewhat glum picture shifts significantly for the worse during the period 2030 to 2050. During these 20 years, overall global demand growth for both the main metals and coal is expected to be much slower, and well below the long-term average for all four commodities. It is a return to the decades of the 1980s and '90s when there was really no engine of the global economy driving metal or coal consumption. The current drivers of the global economy – China and India and to a lesser extent the Advanced Countries – will have all reached their peak of metal demand growth around 2030. As for coal, demand will not only slow down, it will go backwards, retreating at 0.8% per year between 2030 and 2050.

Table 4.11 (above) showed the forecast for total metal consumption. Table 4.12 shows the forecast for mined metal consumption. The two are not the same because of the growing influence of end-of-life scrap. This source of supply will become an increasingly important part of the global metal mix as the years go on.

Table 4.12: Forecast for global metalliferous ore and coal consumption.

		2015	**2030**	**2050**	**Annual inc 2015-30**	**Annual inc 2030-50**	**2050 % of 2015**
Mined copper	Mt/a	19	28	26	2.6%	-0.4%	133%
Bauxite	Mt/a	299	480	410	3.2%	-0.8%	137%
Iron ore	Mt/a	2038	2334	1686	1.0%	-1.6%	83%
Coal	Mt/a	7592	7423	6252	-0.1%	-0.8%	82%

As can be seen from the table, the forecast for the period 2015 to 2030 is for consumption of mined copper, bauxite and iron ore to rise at about the same rate as metal production. In other words, the demand growth rate for mined metal is little different to total metal over the period.

That changes markedly in the period 2030 to 2050. During that 20-year period, the growth rate in the production of mined ore falls well below that of finished metal. Indeed, the already subdued global forecast for metal demand growth turns into a rather grim outlook for mine production. Because at the same time as global metal demand growth is slowing, a lot of scrap is coming onto the market. This pushes all three of the main metalliferous ores into retreat from 2030 to 2050. It is an historically unprecedented downward trend in global mine production. Global production of iron ore in 2050 is well below its level in 2015. Even bauxite production falls between 2030 and 2050. Coal too is a very poor performer over the period, but that would be expected by nearly everyone.

Table 4.13 puts the coming 30 years into historical perspective. If this forecast does come to pass it will be the third period of low demand since the industrial age began in the 1870s. It is not the worst of the three, the Great Depression still claims that distinction.

But the forecast for the coming thirty years, especially in the period 2030 to 2050, is well below what was seen in the other low growth period, 1975-2000.

Table 4.13: Periods of high and low demand since 1900 (average annual growth rate).

	1900-29	1929-38	1950-76	1976-00	2000-15	2015-50
Steel	5.1	(0.3)	5.2	0.9	4.4	0.9
Copper	4.8	0.1	4.6	2.5	2.9	1.8
Aluminium	13.4	9.4	8.6	2.8	5.4	2.1
Coal	2.2	(0.6)	2.4	1.6	3.1	(0.6)
Overall	High	Low	High	Low	High	Low

This being the case, it seems reasonable to expect that prices will fall to the same lows as were reached during the two other slow growth periods. They could fall even further than that. This is because never before in history will recycled metal be contributing so much to the total supply of metal. Given this, there may well be an unprecedented over-supply of metalliferous ores. If that happens, prices will be driven even lower than the levels in the previous two weak periods. But that all depends on what the supply side will do. Which inevitably raises the question: how is the supply side likely to respond over the next thirty years?

Chapter 2

MINERAL SUPPLY TO 2050

The Global Production Base

Having, in the previous chapter, established a forecast for metal and coal demand in 2050, this chapter will be devoted to gaining an understanding of how that demand might be supplied.

Before delving into the sectoral supply outlooks, it is worth looking at the sweep of history when it comes to the supply of minerals. Earlier in this book, it was discussed how the global mining industry has been subject to lengthy periods of high demand growth followed by similarly lengthy periods of low demand growth then back again to high demand growth and so on.

The periods of high demand growth inevitably result in a great deal of pressure being placed upon the global mineral production base. Typically what is being asked of the existing production base cannot be supplied, so new fields are needed.

This was true of the first rapid growth period, between 1880 and 1930. The established fields of Europe were quickly found wanting and it led to the great mineral fields of North America being brought into full production. The copper of the American West, the iron ore of the Mesabi Range and the coking coal of Pennsylvania all rose from almost nothing in 1880 to become mining regions of global pre-eminence by 1910.

This was also true of the second rapid growth period from 1950 to the mid 1970s when the copper fields of the Andes, the South Pacific and the Copperbelt were greatly expanded, the iron ore regions of Pilbara and Minas Gerais were brought on-stream as were the bauxite and coal mines of Australia.

Things have been different so far in the most recent rapid growth period – the China mining boom. There has not yet been much development of new fields of global importance. In iron ore, there has been a massive expansion of the existing Pilbara operations. In bauxite there have been unsustainable expansions in China and Indonesia. And in copper, there have been equally unsustainable expansions in China as well as a revival of the Copperbelt. Overall, the global miners have found it harder than in previous high growth periods to come up with new sources of supply.

They have also found it difficult to develop technical breakthroughs to assist production. It should be noted this is not a new thing. The great days of the technical advance in mining were undoubtedly the first period of high demand growth, from 1880 to 1930. In this period technical breakthroughs abounded. One such, the Gilchrist-Thomas process for phosphorous removal, made available what were previously great swathes of unusable high-phosphorus iron ore in Alsace-Lorraine. Another, mineral flotation, had by 1920 lifted by 25% or so the production possible from each tonne dug out of the world's copper and other base metals mines. Added to developments such as these, between 1890 and 1910 two entirely new metals were brought into commercial production. One was nickel, the other aluminium.

Since then breakthroughs have been few and far between. Instead the mining flowsheet has been improved by a steady accumulation of incremental improvements in the size of machinery, the effectiveness of mineral extraction techniques, the accuracy of measurement and the speed of communication. Computers and computer modelling have made an impact. In fact, advances in computer capability have led in this recent period of high growth to some genuine breakthroughs. These have been in the field of equipment automation, especially of ore haulage trucks. In time these advances will revolutionise the way mining is done.

But the impact of automation on production tonnages has so far been insignificant on the global scale. Which means that during this most recent period of high demand growth, the world's miners have had to make do with the same mining fields and more-or-less the same mining and extraction technologies as they had in the quiet years before it began. This is not a sustainable state of affairs. The global mining production base will have to be renewed with new fields and new production techniques if there is to be any prospect of it supplying yet another high demand growth period.

This renewal, however, is unlikely to happen during the next thirty years because the pressure, for the most part, is off. The coming period of oversupply means that new fields and new production-enhancing technologies will take a backseat.

In the next four chapters, the 30-year supply outlooks for the four sectors of iron ore, coal, bauxite and copper will be discussed. Before doing that, a digression into the history of industrial revolutions will help provide a foundation for the discussion of future technological change.

The Industrial Revolutions

There have so far been three industrial revolutions. 100 years separated the first from the second, then 80 years separated the second from the third. The third took place in 1960. Another 60 years have elapsed since then. So it seems fair to say that within next decade or two the fourth industrial revolution will see the light of day.

The first industrial revolution

The first industrial revolution started with the invention of the Watt steam engine. The steam engine itself was certainly not new by the time James Watt came along. It had been in use in pumping applications since the late 1600s. It may be wondered, then, why it took nearly 100 hundred years for it to move from the narrow field of pumping to the wider world of manufacturing industry. That was because the pre-Watt steam engines had mode of operation which was suited to pumping but hardly anything else. The engines had a "waiting-waiting-waiting then sudden movement" cycle. The "waiting-waiting-waiting" part of the cycle took place while the water in the boiler was turned into steam. The "sudden movement" part of the cycle happened when that steam was condensed in one violent implosion. The sudden condensing of the steam created a vacuum which sucked water up a vertical pipe.

This mode of operation made these early steam engines fairly effective pumps, but they were useless for most other purposes. Most machines operate on a smooth and repetitive cycle, usually at a steady rhythm which can be slowed down or speeded up. The pre-Watt steam engines did not even come to close to having that capability. The reason the Watt steam engine started an industrial revolution was because James Watt's design changes had by 1780 created a new style of steam engine which could produce a steady rotating motion. When this smoothly rotating engine was applied in England's textile mills, the resulting increase in factory productivity propelled the country to the forefront of global manufacturing.

The first industrial revolution had run its course by 1810. By then the steam engine could be found all over Europe and even high in the Andes. It had become a standard fixture in the better-equipped factories of England.

The second industrial revolution

There was a steady improvement of the steam engine over the decades which followed such that it had become quite a formidable machine by the 1880s. A few large steam engines harnessed together were all that was needed to haul long wagon trains across the North American continent. But just as it reached this pinnacle of performance, the steam engine ran headlong into competition from two completely new engines. It lost the struggle against these newcomers, and by the 1920s it was obsolete technology.

The two engines which rendered the steam engine obsolete were the internal combustion engine and the electric dynamo. They hadn't come out of nowhere. Rudimentary models of both were working by the 1830s. The challenge, as it had been with the steam engine, had been to build them so that they could produce reliable, smooth and rapid rotational power, instead of jerky back and forth motion which was their initial mode. After many attempts, success for both came at the same time. Nikolaus Otto made the first public demonstration of his internal combustion engine in 1876, and that was also the year that Charles Brush unveiled his electric dynamo. For that reason, 1876 can be called the first year of the second industrial revolution.[17]

The second industrial revolution was different from the first. The impact of the Watt engine was to greatly improve existing manufacturing processes by making them faster and cheaper. It also led to some other inventions, most importantly the steam locomotive. In contrast, the appearance of the Otto Engine and the Brush Dynamo unleashed a tidal wave of invention. Especially when they were joined by Thomas Edison's invention of the central power station and power distribution grid.

There were reasons for why the second industrial revolution bore so much more fruit than did the first. To start with, electricity (for the dynamo) and petroleum (for the internal combustion engine) were much better sources of energy than the wood and coal used for the steam engine. They provided a far more versatile set of options for running machinery.

In addition to that, during the previous one hundred years there had been a great accumulation of knowledge in the fields of chemistry, electricity, electrolysis, mechanics, metallurgy and physics. By 1880 there were thousands of new ideas for products and machines just waiting for some suitable source of power to bring them to life. There had also been a great proliferation of technical schools and publications such that by 1880 even farm workers could know of the latest scientific developments and challenges. The result was that there were a lot more minds ready to work on whatever problems and opportunities were out there.

So fruitful was the second industrial revolution that by 1920 the industrial and domestic world which had come into being was using most of the mechanical, electrical and chemical techniques and products which are still in use today. The automobile, the refrigerator and the electric light were just three of the ground-breaking inventions which had entered the mainstream of life. The Haber process and many other fundamental chemical techniques had been created and were in operation. There were electricity and telephone networks serving the cities, there were steel-framed high rise office blocks with elevators, there were assembly line factories and there was even airline travel. Modern industry and the modern household had come into being by the time the First World War broke out.

So too had the modern mining industry. Where once there had been prospector's picks, black powder, hammers and bars, mule-drawn barrows, steam-driven stamp mills and shaking tables, and mercury-based extraction of gold, there were now diamond-tipped drills, pneumatic drills, dynamite, steam-driven shovels, electric motor-driven gyrating crushers and rotating ball mills, cyanidation, magnetic separators and rake classifiers. To top it all off there was a miraculous new process called flotation.

The capabilities – size, strength, speed, operating range and precision – of these machines and techniques has greatly improved over the last hundred years. There have also been two new types of engine: jet propulsion and the step motor. And two new energy sources have been harnessed: nuclear and solar. But there has, so far, been no new wave of invention involving physical machinery and chemical processes.

The third industrial revolution

Missing from the modern household in 1920 were the computers, mobile phones and other electronic devices which are now so pervasive. Actually, they were not entirely missing. By 1910, the radio was in regular use on the British naval vessels. Most American households had a radio by 1925. They operated by harnessing, with the help of vacuum tubes, transmitted electromagnetic radiation.

The vacuum tube was an effective device when used in appliances which needed not too many of them. The trouble was that machines which needed a lot of them – especially the early mainframe computers – were overly large, generated a lot of heat, and were prone to failure. So as time went on, it became clearer that the vacuum tube was not up to the task which was being asked of it. It was holding back progress. Which is why the invention which kick-started the third industrial revolution was a replacement for the vacuum tube. It was called the transistor.

The idea of the transistor first saw the light of day during the 1920s, but the first functioning model was built at the Bell Telephone Laboratories in New Jersey in 1947 by John Bardeen and Walter Brattain, working in a team led by William Shockley. Like the vacuum tube, the transistor had the ability to conduct electromagnetic radiation in just one direction, and so was called a semi-conductor. It was much smaller than the vacuum tube, used a lot less energy and generated almost no heat. In other words, it was a much better vacuum tube than the vacuum tube. In 1955 was built the first computer which used mainly transistors, as opposed to mainly vacuum tubes. Then in 1959 came an improved transistor. It was called the MOSFET, or the Metal Oxide Semiconductor Field Effect Transistor. This device remains the basic building block of the computer and the mobile phone. With the MOSFET, the modern world of computing and telecommunications was born.

It took about three decades for the computer to be brought to the mainstream of economic life, just as it had taken about three decades for the steam engine to become widespread, and about the same amount of time for the electric motor and internal combustion engine to find their way onto the factory floors and the open roads. By 1990 the desktop computer was commonplace in offices throughout the Advanced Countries. Mobile phones took a bit longer. They were in widespread use by the end of that decade.

Computing speed has greatly advanced since the early days. So has the computing power which can be packed into a small package. In 1977, the state-of-the-art IBM microprocessor held some 10,000 transistors. In 2017, IBM released a silicon chip which held 30 billion of them. Computational speed is one thing, the capability of computers and mobile phones is another. This has advanced rapidly too. They have shifted from being machines used to do calculations to machines which can monitor the environment and take actions in response to changes in that environment. Within ten years from now, a computer will be able to drive a vehicle in real-world road conditions, dealing with bad weather, poor light and careless road-users just as well as a human could.

This shift to robotic machinery and thinking computers has been called the fourth industrial revolution.[18] Yet it is not an industrial revolution. An industrial revolution begins with the invention of a disruptive new technology. In the last three industrial revolutions the disruptive technologies have been the Watt steam engine, the Otto internal combustion engine and the Brush electric dynamo, and the MOSFET. Today's shift to robotic control of machinery does not rest on a disruptive technology. Instead, it relies on the integration of a range of existing technologies. All the advances of the previous twenty years are being brought together. It is more accurate, and useful, to say that what is happening today is the second stage of the third industrial revolution.

It is worth elaborating on this notion of stages of industrial revolutions. The fact is that all the industrial revolutions have unfolded in two stages. The first industrial revolution began with the Watt steam engine, then its second stage was defined by the building of continent-wide railway networks along which travelled thousands of steam-driven locomotives carrying products of city-based factories to all the markets of the country, co-ordinated by the telegraph and controlled by industrial bureaucracies.

The second industrial revolution began with the Otto internal combustion engine and the Brush electric dynamo, then its second stage was defined by the development of electrically-powered factories, connected to each other by telephone networks, and with each factory organised around conveyor belt-driven assembly lines which were relentlessly improved by time and motion studies.

The third industrial revolution began with the MOSFET, and its second stage is being defined by the development of robotically-controlled machinery and thinking computers which are networked together using the internet, WiFi and GPS and continually optimised using the data collected from the previous day's operation.

The fourth industrial revolution

The first industrial revolution started in 1780, the second in 1880 and the third in 1960. The interval between first and second was 100 years, between the second and third it was 80 years. It has now been 60 years since the invention of the MOSFET. It seems to be only a matter of a few decades before the fourth industrial revolution will be starting to transform the economies of the

> Advanced Countries. What disruptive technology will be at the heart of it? The history of industrial revolutions suggests that it is a technology already known about but (a) does not work very well, or (b) cannot be built very well with existing techniques.
>
> It is obviously speculation, but one possibility is that the fourth industrial revolution could be driven by a pair of disruptive technologies: a much more efficient solar panel, and a much higher performance battery. There is plenty of work going on in both these areas, driven by the desire to use the intermittent clean energy sources of solar and wind. This combination of highly efficient solar energy production coupled with highly effective energy storage would create a very low-cost source of energy, available around the clock. With this inexhaustible supply of very cheap baseload energy, the industrial processes currently in use may well be transformed into a completely new set. After all, nearly every industrial technology has been designed with minimising energy consumption as one important constraint. Should that constraint be lifted, a whole new look would be taken at the world's industrial processes. It would be the second industrial revolution all over again.

Iron Ore to Steel

After that diversion into the history and possible future of industrial technology, it is now time to look at how the four main mineral sectors may develop to 2050. The starting point will be global iron ore.

The total world production of iron ore in 2018 was well over double what it was in 2003. Half of the increased production came from the Pilbara, and most of the rest came from Brazil, China and India. The other global regions were minor participants or not really participants at all.

Before considering what will be needed in the future, it is worth repeating a point which has been noted earlier. Of these four producing regions only one of them – the Pilbara – has been a significant contributor to the increase in global iron ore production in the last ten years. In fact, the Pilbara has contributed nearly all of the increase in global iron ore production in the last ten years. The rest of the global production platform hit the limits ten years ago either of its resources (China), its infrastructure capability (Brazil) or its licence to operate (India). Only the Pilbara had plenty left to draw upon with respect to all three of these, and so it alone has supplied the raw iron units for the world's additional steel production since 2008.

Given this, in considering how the global iron ore sector may evolve over the next thirty years, one question to be asked is: can the Pilbara continue to supply all of the world's new demand up until the 2030s (after which demand starts to fall)? The forecast in the previous chapter has global iron ore demand rising by some 400 million tonnes between 2020 and 2030, which is less than the increase in shipments between 2010 and 2020. Which means that the Pilbara has already proven itself capable of supplying the required additional iron ore tonnage to 2030.

That is hardly a guarantee that it can do it again of course. For the Pilbara producers to achieve this, they need to (a) get more iron ore through the existing rail and port infrastructure, and then (b) identify and build new rail and port expansion capacity. Looking first at getting more ore through existing rail and port capacity, the effort to do this has been at the top of the agenda for quite some time. The transition to driver-less trains is one big part of it and is expected to deliver significant gains. That will be an important contribution but driver-less trains and other automation initiatives, along with improved scheduling, will not be enough to deliver the needed 40% increase in shipped tonnages. The rest will have to come from additional rail and port capacity. Whether this can be done has not been confirmed by the producers, so the true expansion potential is not publicly known. Still, it seems a fair assumption that there is still, say, a 30% expansion capability given enough incentive. So, the answer to the question posed above is: yes, the Pilbara can supply, if not all, then a very substantial part of the world's additional iron ore requirements to 2030.

Having reached that conclusion, it will surely be the case that the Pilbara will not be the sole source of new iron ore capacity to 2030. For one thing, the region's ore grades are falling and the world's steelmakers would not want to rely solely on extra supplies of lower grade ore. Which is why the Simandou project in Guinea is of so much interest. Its attraction comes from the fact that it is a big deposit containing ore which is very high grade. The current indicative mine plan is for production of 100 million tonnes per year of ore with 65% iron content. At these tonnages it will be a meaningful source of blending ore to overcome the falling grades from the Pilbara.

Simandou is not the only source of high grade ore which could help manage the Pilbara grade decline. There are other prospects in West Africa and then there are the Brazilian deposits, especially in the Amazon Basin where there is expansion potential. The pellets made from these ores are even higher grade than Simandou's run-of-mine ore, so there will be renewed interest in them. In India, there are also high grade ores, particularly in the "southern system" deposits in Karnataka and Goa. All of which means that the likely situation in 2030 will be that the Pilbara will provide most of the new supply, and its ores will be supplemented by a mixture of new West African, Brazilian and Indian ore production capacity.

The decade to 2030 will probably be something like business as usual in global iron ore and steel. Production growth should be about 2% per year, well below the heady heights of the China boom but somewhere near the long-term average. After 2030, however, it will be far from business as usual. Three factors will combine to drive change in the industry.

1. The first of these is the increasing severity of global warming and the subsequent increasing pressure to do something about CO_2 emissions. The blast furnace steelmaking process is estimated to produce about 8% of the world's CO_2 emissions caused by the burning of fossil fuels. This will bring it plenty of adverse attention in the decades to come.

2. The second factor driving change is that China's steel consumption will likely have stopped growing by 2030, and India's will also be peaking. Pushing in the opposite direction is South East Asia, where steel consumption is expected to double between 2030 and 2050. But that will not nearly compensate for the loss of China as a growth engine.
3. The third factor is that China's cities will be beginning a new career as urban mines. The first signs will be appearing of what will eventually become a very large supply of end-of-life steel. By 2050, China's production of this end-of-life steel will have grown so large that the country will have shuttered about half of its of blast furnace steelmaking capacity unless export markets can be found.

With these factors bearing down on global steelmaking, the period 2030 to 2050 will see the creation of a very different sector.

To begin with, about one third of global blast furnace capacity will be closed. Most of this will be in the Advanced Countries and in China. It is likely that virtually all capacity in the Advanced Countries will be shuttered, and China will lose about one quarter of its capacity.

But that will still leave 900 million tonnes of steel potentially being produced by the CO_2 emissions-intensive blast furnace route. That will bring the steelmakers plenty of scrutiny. They will probably respond by moving to lower emissions pathways for the production of pig iron. There are two of them.

The first is known as the direct reduction of iron ore, or DRI. It has been in commercial use for many years but is a relatively high cost operation and, as of 2020, less than one in ten tonnes of the world's iron ore is processed that way. The process goes like this: the iron ore is ground down to a sandy consistency, it is then rolled into marble-sized pellets which are baked in a rotary kiln. These baked pellets are then packed into a vertical kiln and subjected to a much fiercer heat amid blast furnace-like conditions. This has the effect of removing most of the oxygen from the pelletised iron ore, thereby creating pellets of (close to) pig iron. These pellets are then melted in an electric arc furnace and the waste elements, such as silica, are removed as slag. This entire process has potentially far lower CO_2 emissions than the blast furnace route. A more recent variation of the DRI process is the Hisarna process. It bypasses the pelletising steps and instead uses a swirling fluidised bed to achieve the iron reduction. If it can be made to work, it will be a significantly cheaper pathway than the standard pellet-based process.

The second low emissions route to pig iron retains the blast furnace but uses hydrogen to replace a good part of the blast furnace coal[19]. It is an attractive option because virtually all of the world's steel is made through the blast furnace process and a large proportion of the blast furnaces, which are very large and capital intensive, have been built in the past 20 years. This means they are still far from retirement age and their owners would be reluctant to close them down. The hydrogen gas replaces the pulverised coal which is injected into the base of the blast furnace. Whilst this would not fully eliminate the CO_2 emissions, it would significantly reduce them. As with Hisarna, it is still a process in development.

Of these two, the hydrogen process would be the easier to implement. Hisarna, and DRI more broadly, is more difficult because it would require building new pig iron production plants during a thirty-year period when there are going to be widespread closures of such plants.

Whichever mix of traditional blast furnace, hydrogen-supplemented blast furnace and DRI/Hisarna comes into being, the majority of this iron ore-based steelmaking will be located in just two regions: China and India. A third, smaller, centre may be developed in the natural gas-rich Gulf States, using the DRI/Hisarna process.

The great majority of iron ore-based steelmaking will probably remain in China alone, and as a result China will become the exporter of end-of-life scrap and finished steel to the world. This would allow it to keep up to three quarters of its blast furnace plants in operation. The reason this is the most likely outcome is that South East Asia has not yet developed much of an iron ore-based steelmaking sector, and it is unlikely to do so post-2030. Instead it will turn to China for its steel, just as China is likely to turn to South East Asia for some of its lower cost manufactured goods.

India may also turn to China for its additional steel, but that seems less likely. It is more likely that India will build its own iron ore-based steelmaking plants, becoming self-sufficient in steel as have many industrialising nations before it. This would also mean becoming self-sufficient, or close to it, in iron ore. It is probably going to be the case that China will remain the global centre of iron ore-based steelmaking, with India a smaller but still substantial contributor.

As for global iron ore, production is forecast to decline by one third between 2030 and 2050, with the result that production in 2050 will be below what it was in 2020. Every iron ore producing country in the world will be affected, but some much more than others. The least affected will be the high grade producers. Simandou (if it ever gets into production) will be one of these. So will the Amazon Basin producers. Indian producers will probably also avoid the worst of it. Low grade producers will suffer the biggest blows. The Mesabi Range will be closed down, and China's once mighty iron ore sector will probably be not much more than a memory. The Pilbara producers will still be the central pillar of global production, particularly if China holds its position as the centre of iron ore-based steelmaking. But production from the Pilbara will be much reduced from the heights reached in the early 2030s. Global iron ore will be a hard-hit industry.

Coal

The outlook for the global production of coal over the next thirty years is for very slow growth to 2030 and then steady decline. It is a similar situation to what is facing iron ore, only coal will be even harder hit.

China will remain the highest coal consuming country of the world. In 2050, it is forecast to burn more than 3 billion tonnes of coal each year in its power stations and industrial furnaces, twice as much as India and three times as much as the Advanced Countries. China's coal mining sector will, as a result, remain the largest in the world, although by then it will have already been in 20 years of slow decline. The centre of gravity of Chinese coal will stay in the Shanxi-Inner Mongolia region, where the known reserves are still very large. By the mid 2030s, it is quite possible that China will have become self-sufficient once more in coal, just as it has been for most of its history. However as the global coal demand-supply balance shifts to oversupply, the high quality coals will win. This trend will favour Australian coal, which may well, therefore, remain in the Chinese mix for decades to come. Indonesia will be the loser in any battle over quality in an over-supplied market.

Turning to the Advanced Countries, coal consumption in 2050 will be less than half of what it is in 2020. The three sub-regions will have different dynamics. In Greater Europe, coal use in the western European countries will be almost completely gone. Further east, the closure rate of coal-fired power stations will likely be much slower, because there will be a reluctance to close coal-fired power stations that are still producing efficiently. As for the supply of coal, the German and Polish coal industries will be much reduced in their output. The German mines will probably be fully shutdown. What coal production remains in Greater Europe will be mostly from the lower-cost mines in Russia, Ukraine and Kazakhstan.

In the North American sub-region, over this past decade coal consumption has been in the same sort of decline as in Greater Europe. Nearly all of the coal used in North America goes into power generation, and coal's contribution in this sector has, in just five years, dropped from nearly 40% to less than 30%. Much of this is due to aging coal-fired power stations being replaced by gas-fired stations thanks to the greatly increased availability of coal seam gas. This trend will probably continue despite the fact that there is more political support for coal, as a traditional blue-collar employer, in the United States than in Greater Europe. So the decline of coal may be slower but by 2050 it will be much-reduced from current levels. Only the lowest cost and best run coal mines will still be in operation.

The East Asian sub-region as of 2020 remains a stronghold of coal-fired power generation. Coal produces more than one third of the electricity used in Japan, South Korea and Taiwan. These countries have been slow to move towards renewable energy. In Japan, when the 2011 tsunami disaster precipitated the closure of the nuclear power stations, LNG and coal-fired power stations were built to replace it, with hardly any wind and solar.

That is changing and the renewable energy sector is starting to become a serious contributor to the electricity generation mix. Indeed, it now seems reasonable to expect that Japan and its neighbours will follow in the path of Greater Europe and North America in pushing coal out of the energy mix. Being dependent on foreign coal imports, imports of coal into the sub-region will continue but it will be a much lower level by 2050. The needed coking coal, much reduced from today's levels, will come from Australian mines, if they are still operating, or Chinese. The Japanese preference for high quality may well mean that they will also stick with Australian thermal coal, again assuming they are still operating, over the Indonesia and Chinese varieties.

In India, the coal sector will present a more dynamic scene. India's coal consumption is expected to rise from about 1 billion tonnes per year to 1.5 billion tonnes between 2020 and 2050. In some respects, India's coal production and delivery system resembles China's. Like in China, the coal resources are concentrated in one part of the country. In India's case, this is the north-eastern corner where the coal is found in three river basins: the Damodar, the Son and the Mahanadi. Like China, the coal resources are also far from the main urban centres. Chennai is at least 1,000 kilometres by rail from the Mahanadi Valley mines. Mumbai is 1,800 kilometres by rail from the Damodar Valley. So, as in China, about three quarters of production is transported by railway over long distances. There is not be enough rolling stock and railway track to deal with this traffic, and the result is severe railway congestion and shortages of coal. This is one reason why Indian coal consumers have turned to imported coal during the past 15 years.

While there are similarities with China, there are also some big differences. The Indian mines are almost all open-cut whereas in China they have always been predominantly underground. Open cut mines are cheaper to operate but it is more difficult to obtain approval for them, because of the greater land disturbance. Another difference between India and China is that India has a poorer quality of coal.

Because of all these rail transport, mine approval and coal quality issues, imported coal is likely to play an even bigger part in India's future than it does now. In the populous and relatively coal-free west coast of India, imported coal will probably be cheaper than domestic. The 60 million tonne per year Carmichael mine project is being built upon this expectation. It is located in the Galilee Basin, a large and hitherto undeveloped coal region in inland north-eastern Australia. Adani, the owner of the project, is an Indian infrastructure group and the biggest privately-owned electricity generator in the country. The company's determination to develop the Carmichael project even in the face of very strong and prolonged environmental opposition demonstrates its view of the future of the Indian domestic coal sector.

By 2050, global coal will have retreated somewhat from the vibrant traded sector that it was at its peak during the 2010s. It will have become a more regional industry. There will be two coal trading zones:

1. The eastern part of Greater Europe where Russian and Ukrainian coal mines will supply the remaining demand from the East European countries. This will be a much-diminished sector.
2. The Pacific and Indian Oceans where Australian, Indonesian and Chinese coal mines will supply baseload tonnages to Japan, South Korea and Taiwan, and baseload and blending coal to India. Depending on the growth of domestic coal production in India, this will be a similar-sized sector to 2020, or perhaps even larger.

A significant unknown is what the Australian coal sector will look like in 2050. Will the Galilee Basin have become a new global production platform feeding India and East Asia? Or will Australian coal have lost its licence to operate? From a global perspective, it would be best to keep the Australian coal mines operating as long as there is significant demand for coal anywhere in the world. This is because, on average, Australian coal is better quality than the rest. If this happens it is quite possible that Australia's coal exports could substantially increase from the 2020 level driven by a coal-hungry west coast of India. The EIA 2019 study forecasts this.

However, policies governing CO_2 emissions reduction are not always based on rational calculation. That is nowhere more evident than in Australia itself, where the past decade has seen sensible energy policy turned into farce by a small but influential group of politicians who saw electoral advantage in exploiting a widely-held, especially amongst older voters, "anti-greenie" sentiment.

The influence of this group is slowly waning and the sentiment in the Australian electorate seems to now be in favour of establishing a set of CO_2 emissions reduction policies which will have long-term impact. If this does come about, it is quite possible that this policy correction pendulum will continue swinging until the country's emissions reduction policies also result in a much tougher stance on its export coal sector.

However that works out, global coal will be a smaller industry in 2050 than it was in 2020, and that is the most favourable outlook. There could be much steeper reductions if the leaders of China and India manage to make good on their public statements and take a much more aggressive approach to CO_2 emissions reduction. Whichever way that goes, by 2050 most countries will be pushing hard to eliminate coal altogether from their energy mix. By 2080 coal, it seems certain, will be the energy equivalent of the steam engine.

Bauxite to Aluminium

The outlook for bauxite over the next thirty years is for 10 or so years of steady growth, and 20 or so years of slow decline. The main driver over the next ten years is the steadily increasing intensity of use in the Advanced Countries and China. The driver of the subsequent decline will be a historically unprecedented surge in the availability of aluminium scrap. This will come about because of Chinese urban rebuilding in the 2030s and 40s which will release back into circulation China's great stock of aluminium which was incorporated into buildings in the 2010s.

In the light of this, one question to consider is: how will the global mix of bauxite production shift over the next thirty years? As of 2020, global bauxite comes mostly from five countries. Australia is still the largest producer, China is in second place, followed by Guinea and Brazil, and then India in fifth place. China imports much of the Australian, Guinean and Brazilian production. It is by far the largest producer of both alumina and aluminium metal.

Things have changed dramatically from the latter years of the mining boom. During those years the bauxite producers of the world were struggling to meet demand. The Chinese mines had about reached their peak, the Indonesian fields had been closed down by the central government in Jakarta, the Australian and Brazilian mines were in the midst of protracted expansion projects, political confusion was holding up half a dozen projects in Guinea, and in Vietnam the national mining company, Vinacomin, was out of its depth in building the country's first bauxite-alumina project.

Five years later and there is a looming oversupply. The causes:

- *Exports have re-started from Indonesia.* In response to the Indonesian government's demands for downstream processing, that country now has five alumina plants either in operation or being constructed. The companies who have built these alumina plants are permitted to export a portion of their bauxite while the alumina capacity is being installed. All of this means that Indonesian bauxite is being produced at 15 million tonnes per year, with much higher production in prospect.
- *New mines have finally opened in Australia.* In the country's North Queensland bauxite fields, a new mine, Amrun, has finally

been commissioned and there have been two other significant capacity expansions. At the opposite end of the country, in the south Western Australian fields, smaller expansions have taken place. All of these were long in coming and never saw the light of the day until well after the China mining boom had ended.

- *Bauxite production is climbing in India.* It has been steadily climbing along with the country's aluminium production. The mines are concentrated in Odisha State which is also where most of the alumina refining and aluminium smelting capacity is. There is plenty of expansion capacity and it is likely that Indian domestic demand will be satisfied by domestic production except for imported manufactured goods containing aluminium.
- *Guinea has undergone a sudden transformation to become a major global producer.* It has shifted from being an onlooker to being a central player on the world bauxite stage. National production of bauxite has risen from 15 million tonnes per year in 2015 to over 60 million tonnes in 2020. In the hyper-expansionist China of the mining boom, it took ten years for bauxite production to do that.

Which raises the question: what happened in Guinea?

Some background is helpful. That Guinea was rich in bauxite had been known since the 1950s.[20] The post-independence President, Sékou Touré, had invited the Soviets to develop an industry. Wishing to expand their political influence in West Africa, the Soviets leapt at the opportunity. They opened a mine and constructed an alumina refinery at Fria, and built a railway from there to the port city of Conakry. It was all up and running by 1960. There was a second burst of activity in the early 1970s when the Guinean government combined with a consortium of six foreign aluminium companies, Alcan and Alcoa among them, to form Compagnie Bauxite de Guinée, or CBG. CBG developed the Sangarédi mine, an export port at Kamsar, and a railway linking them. The bauxite was shipped to foreign refineries. It was the largest exporting mine in the world.

That is how the situation stayed for forty years. President Touré died in office in 1984, after a reign of 36 years. He was succeeded by Lansana Conté, who held the office for 24 years, dying while still President in 2008. Both of these men were typical of African heads of state of the time. As a first generation leader, Touré made some attempts at developing domestic industry before giving it up when the western world hit recession in the 1970s and holding on to power with grim determination. Conté, as a second generation leader, came to power in a military coup, let the IMF dictate his economic policy, re-introduced democracy in the 1990s and, like his predecessor, hung on to power however he could. He was succeeded by Alpha Condé.

When the China mining boom swept across the world, Guinea stayed on the sidelines. Through the ten years of the boom, the country was stuck in the final years of the Conté regime and then distracted by the first chaotic years of the Condé regime. Foreign mining companies knew the country well but no development was undertaken because corruption was at world-class levels and the rules for investment kept changing. The low point was reached when metal prices dropped in 2012. Rusal, the successor to the Soviets, closed its Fria refinery, and BHP Billiton walked away from Boffa and Santou-Houda, two of the country's best bauxite deposits.[21] At that point there were just two operating mines: Sangarédi, which was started in 1973, and Kindia, which began operations in 1974. Annual production had hardly changed in forty years.

What has happened since has been remarkable. When the Indonesian bauxite fields were closed down a new look was taken at Guinea. It was known to be a bauxite field ready to go. At least a dozen foreign mining companies had been camped in the country for years, some had been there for decades. Which is to say Guinea was very well understood technically and logistically. Standing in the way of investment was political risk. With the loss of Indonesia, however, the game changed. President Condé came under renewed pressure to improve the investment climate, and eventually did take some steps in that direction. More importantly, the foreign companies changed their attitude to the political risk and shifted from conducting feasibility studies to becoming investors.

They were a diverse group. There were global majors, including Chalco and Rusal, and juniors developing their first mine, such as UK-based Alufer and Australia's AMC. Other state-owned companies were there too. The UAE-owned Guinea Alumina Corporation acquired the rights to the Boke mine and undertook to build an alumina refinery, and a Chinese consortium took on BHP's abandoned Santou-Houda deposit, promising to build a railway from deep in the interior. Projects were in construction by 2015, the first greenfields developments since the 1970s. The result was that, in the space of four years, from 2017 to 2020, six new mines came on-stream. Guinea had gone from being the lost opportunity in global bauxite, to being a heavy-weight producer, with the capability of playing a big part in the next thirty years.

The emergence of Guinea, along with the revival of Indonesia and a new-generation of projects in Australia, has reinvigorated the global bauxite production platform. It is being strengthened even further by the development of Vietnam's Central Highlands deposits and the steady build-up of Indian capacity. All of which means that there are plenty of sources of new production through to the 2030s. There will be no shortage of global bauxite over the next ten years.

There is a critical assumption underpinning that statement. The assumption is that Indonesia, Guinea, Vietnam and India maintain steady policies regarding the development and export of their domestic mineral resources. Which in turn probably means that a substantial base of alumina refining capacity will be built within those countries. This is because all four of them have a history of resource nationalism, meaning they will insist upon the domestic processing of minerals before exporting them.

This likely surplus of bauxite will increase after 2030. Aluminium scrap will supply all of the new demand post-2030 and will start to displace bauxite from its already existing customers. It is likely that the mines of Brazil, Jamaica and Australia will be most impacted by this declining demand environment. This is because the strongest consuming regions – India, China, and South East Asia – will have their own domestic sources to draw on and these domestic mines will receive priority over imported bauxite. Guinea, with its state-owned foreign investors, will also likely receive priority as a source of imports into the investor countries.

As for the world's refinery and smelting capacity, on the refining side of things there will be widespread closures of older plants in China and some construction of new capacity in India and South East Asia. And China will probably lose a good part of its smelting capacity. As for the core processing pathway, unlike in steel where coal is used in the core process, there will be no particular pressure brought to bear to change the basic technologies for aluminium. The bauxite, alumina and primary aluminium sectors will be treading water from 2030, but at least they will avoid the widespread closures which will happen in iron ore and coal.

Copper Ore to Metal

For the next 10 years, the demand for copper will probably continue to outstrip the ability of the global production platform to supply it. By how much is the big unknown. At one end of the possibility spectrum is undersupply so severe that, to misquote Robert Friedland, "you are going to need a telescope to see copper prices in 2030."[22] At the other end is a nearly balanced market, with supply just managing to keep pace with demand. It will probably all come down to how quickly the Copperbelt manages to increase production.

Looking at the demand side first, according to the forecast, over the next ten years about 450,000 tonnes of new mined copper capacity has to be added every year to meet demand. Meaning that the annual tonnage of mined copper will have to increase by 4.5 million tonnes in ten years. That is not all that much more than was actually added each decade between 1990 and 2020. So the first observation which may be made is that keeping pace with demand over the next ten years seems within the capability of the global production system. Yet a look at each of the main copper mining regions of the world suggests that, without a strong performance from the Copperbelt, global copper production will once again lag well behind demand.

To take each region in turn:

The Andes

In the Andes, the outlook for a substantial production increase to 2030, or even much increase at all, is not promising. There are many large projects being studied in the region, but not many of them look like making the leap from the desktop study to construction stage. The trouble is that new Andean mine developments have become prohibitively expensive. They have always been expensive but in the last ten years or so the upfront capital cost of a new mine has gone up by a factor of three to five.

Two things drive this. Firstly, the easiest to develop of the deposits are already in production. Those which remain have lower head grades, deeper orebodies and more difficult locations. Which means that they need much more capital per annual tonne. Secondly the once abundant supplies of fresh water and hydropower in northern Chile are mostly taken, so most of the new mine developments have to put money aside for a sizeable desalination plant and a large power plant run on wind, solar or hydropower.

The four largest new projects – the Chuquicamata Underground, El Teniente's New Mine Level (or NML) project, El Abra's Sulfolix and the Quebrada Blanca Stage II – are aimed at extending the life of existing mines.[23] None are designed to produce more copper.

There are some new developments planned. Rio Blanco is one, and Quellaveco is another, and then there are any number of incremental expansions which will take place throughout the region. But most of the time and money scheduled to be invested into Andean copper over the next ten years is aimed at replacing exhausted mining areas, or counteracting head grade decline. These kinds of projects are viable because they use existing infrastructure. Brand new projects, needing new infrastructure, are a very different matter. As a result, there is little production growth in sight.

The South Pacific

The outlook is somewhat brighter in the South Pacific, but here also a lot of uncertainty surrounds the two largest potential developments. One of those is the Olympic Dam Brownfields Expansion Project, which would nearly double the current mine production. The plan is to convert the existing underground operation to a very large open pit. This project has been under active consideration for over a decade and has been deferred twice, the second time because the development capital cost of US$20 billion was far too great. That was in 2012. Since then, the search has been on for lower cost way of doing it. No satisfactory plan has yet emerged.

The other project is Tampakan in the Philippines. Whilst not quite in the same category as Olympic Dam, Tampakan is also in the upper echelon of global copper deposits. It too has been under consideration for over a decade, and like the Olympic Dam expansion project is very expensive to develop. The hold-up in this case is environmental approvals. They have been withheld because many Filipino politicians, including the current President, have a distrust of open pit mining given the adverse impacts of such mines some 20 years ago.

These projects are needed if any output growth is to happen in the region. This is partly because the biggest producer in the region, the Grasberg mine in Indonesia, is now in life-extension mode. A block caving operation was opened in 2019 to replace the open-pit. Mining is also planned to move into several adjacent orebodies over the next five years. Overall production will increase only marginally.

It seems likely that Olympic Dam and Tampakan will eventually proceed at some time during the next decade, thereby adding perhaps some 500,000 tonnes of annual production capacity. That is probably the best that can be hoped for.

China, Greater Europe and North America

As for China, Greater Europe and North America, production seems at best likely to hold steady in the next five years. There are large projects on the drawing board in all of these regions. The closest to becoming firm development proposals appear to be the Resolution and Pebble projects in North America. The first of these, Resolution, is a very deep but high-grade deposit located underneath the now-abandoned Magma Copper mine in Arizona. The other, the Pebble Mine project, is lower grade and somewhat closer to the surface. Both projects have been in the slow lane as far as development goes, hampered by environmental concerns, high capital cost and engineering complexity. The fact that they are the brightest hopes of these regions is a telling indicator of just how difficult large projects are to develop.

The Copperbelt

Which brings us to the Copperbelt. In 2020, the region's production of mined copper was about 2 million tonnes per year, which was 10% of the global total. There is a reasonable expectation that this could double over the next ten years. The current development outlook for the Copperbelt is for an average of about 200,000 tonnes of mined copper to come on-stream each year to 2030, and that would add a total of 2 million tonnes per year by 2030. About half of this is expected to come from the Kamoa-Kakula deposit alone, which is expected to produce its first concentrate in 2021. The rest is from a combination of new mines and expansions of existing mines.

The copper resources of the region are "sediment-hosted" deposits. Sediment-hosted deposits are usually much higher grade than porphyry deposits, often averaging over 2% copper content in the ore. They are also usually much smaller in terms of total contained copper than porphyry deposits. But not always. In the Copperbelt, some very large deposits have been found. One of them is Tenke Fungurume, lying west of Kolwezi in the Democratic Republic of the Congo. Another is its near neighbour, and the wunderkind of the sediment-hosted world, the Kamoa-Kakula project. Kamoa-Kakula is said to have over a billion tonnes of ore containing an average of about 2.7% copper.[24]

But there is still more potential within the Copperbelt. It is a highly prospective region. Kamoa-Kakula is an example of what lurks beneath the surface. It is a recent discovery, having been first drilled in 2009, and this raises the prospect of other such deposits lying below the surface just awaiting the geologist's drill. With a few more high-grade, near-to-surface discoveries, and a high copper price driving those discoveries into production, the Copperbelt could add substantially more than the expected 2 million tonne increase.

That is the optimistic way of looking at the future for the Copperbelt. There are several ways it could all go wrong. One is the failure of Kamoa-Kakula to meet its production forecasts. A second is the failure to find any more substantial orebodies. Still another risk is the political situation. Kolwezi is 2,000 kilometres from the capital, Kinshasa. It is highly vulnerable to being overrun by rebels should fighting escalate once again. Even if the Copperbelt remains free of violence, the copper mines and their owners still face the risk of adverse shifts in policy, driven by budget emergencies, changes in political direction or mere changes of mind in the senior ranks of the country's political leadership. One victim of a recent change in political direction was First Quantum Minerals. It departed the Congo in 2012, having fallen foul of the DRC government by standing its ground when the government was seeking to renegotiate mining lease agreements.

The prospects of the global supply of copper meeting global demand rest upon (a) a strong showing from Kamoa-Kakula (b) further exploration finds in the Copperbelt which are quickly turned into operating mines and (c) a continuing stable political situation in the DRC and Zambia. This is a lot to ask of single region with a chequered history. The likelihood, therefore, is for a significant global copper shortage to 2030, just as there has been since 2005.

After 2030

After about 2030, the "urban mines" of China will start ramping-up their production and their output will grow steadily over the next

20 years. That will take the pressure off the actual mine production platform, and have the effect of ensuring that the global copper market is in some sort of balance by the 2040s.

The post-2030 period may also see an acceleration in the rate of new projects coming on-stream. After all, there is no shortage of known copper deposits around the world. In the Copperbelt and the Andes, there is something approaching 1,000 million tonnes of undeveloped copper resources. To this can be added the USGS-assessed porphyry resources of North America (300Mt), the Indonesian Archipelago (100Mt), the Balkans and Armenia (120Mt) and Central Asia, stretching across Kazakhstan and Mongolia, (110Mt). And to this can be added various other known sediment-hosted copper deposits across the world, amounting to about 130Mt, and a scattering of other porphyry deposits. In total, the USGS assessment is that about 1,600 million tonnes of identified copper contained in orebodies which are not yet in production.[25]

All of them face significant development challenges, because all have some combination of high political risk, low grades, poor water availability, unsuitable geomechanics (for block caving) and high engineering difficulty. Technological advances, particularly in the field of robotic mining equipment, may lower the difficulty of developing some of these orebodies. Indeed, it is in the deep block-cave copper mines of the Andes and elsewhere that the advances in mine vehicle robotics may well have their greatest impact. Which in turn may result in faster growing mined copper production after 2030.

So the post-2030 period may turn out to be one of more plentiful copper than the 2000 to 2030 period. Even so, of the four sectors examined here, copper will be the only one where supply will be hard-pressed to meet demand during the decades of downturn: the 2030s and 40s.

The Mine of the Future

If anything in the technological sphere can be a sure thing, then it is a sure thing that in the course of the next thirty years most of the mines and processing plants of the world will become robotically operated, with people overseeing the operations but taking little active part in their operation. There have already been successful attempts to employ driver-less trains, trucks and digging machines in mining operations. Things are moving forward from there. There has now been constructed an entire mining operation – the Syama underground development in Mali – which uses only robotic machinery. This is the first mining operation where the operations are designed to be run by robotic machines, also known as autonomous machines, which "talk" to each other and make their own adjustments to their operating practice on the basis of real-time conditions.

There will no doubt be plenty of teething problems with Syama, and plenty of human intervention. The problems will eventually be overcome, and it seems a good bet that it will be running as intended by the mid 2020s give or take a few years. Syama will surely be followed by others before 2030 but it is likely that the adoption of fully-robotic mining will be slower than might be expected. Open pit operations will be the easiest test-beds for the new technology, as will completely new mines or mine extensions. Existing operations – especially underground – will be a lot slower to adopt the technology. But when the whole concept has been fully tested and proven, the operator-free underground mine will become the standard way of doing things. This transition will probably have been completed by the mid 2040s.

The robot-run mine will be the most far-reaching change in mining operations over the next thirty years. It will not be the only one. Water consumption will receive plenty of attention. Water will be a scarce, or begrudged, resource in many mines and processing plants, and this will result in plenty of pressure to find ways to mine ore without disturbing the water table, and to concentrate ores without using hydrometallurgical techniques. In response, amphibious robotic mining machinery will make an appearance before 2050, and the standard mine-to-mill flowsheet will develop in the water-less direction. Pneumatic separation techniques will progressively takeover from hydraulic. And as energy becomes cheaper, pyrometallurgical techniques will move upstream into the processing stages once considered the preserve of hydrometallurgy.

This evolution will be slow, because that has been the tempo of flowsheet evolution for the past hundred years. That tempo will change if tough stances are taken by regulatory authorities. One possibility is the refusal to grant, or renew, permits to operations which incorporate tailings dams. This sort of move seems sure to come, although the timing is a matter of speculation. But some speculation will be permitted because this is the final section of this book. What if the 2050s sees two developments:

- the world-wide phasing out of tailings dams due to water shortages made worse by the impact of global warming, and
- the fourth industrial revolution, driven by the invention of far more effective solar capture and energy storage devices which guarantee almost-free energy on demand.

Together these two developments would drive radical changes to the mine-mill-smelter flowsheet, creating the same degree of transformation which occurred during the second industrial revolution. If this comes about, and so does a revival in the global demand for metals as global warming-driven urban restructuring moves into top gear, the mining industry post-2050 will be a dynamic place for those still working in it.

References

1 *The Path of Industrialisation: 1880 to 2050,* Martin Lynch, InHouse Publishing, 2021

2 *The Stages of Economic Growth: a Non-Communist Manifesto,* Walt Whitman Rostow, Cambridge University Press, 1960

3 *Steel Statistical Yearbook 1980,* International Iron and Steel Institute, 1980

4 *Historical Statistics for Minerals and Materials in the United States,* Thomas D Kelly and Grecia R Matos, United States Geological Survey, 2014

5 *The automobile and the environment in American history,* Martin V Melosi, Automobile in American Life and Society website

6 *Automotive Industry Outlook,* Mike Wall, HIS Markit Conference, February 2019

7 *Copper versus aluminium induction – motor rotor: which one is best?* M Hodowanec, IEEE Industry Applications Magazine, August 2002

8 *The US Copper-base Scrap Industry and its By-products – 2006,* Copper Development Association, February 2007

9 *World Steel Recycling in Figures, 2012-2016,* Bureau of International Recycling Ferrous Division, 2017

10 *Automotive aluminium recycling at end of life: a grave-to-gate analysis,* Sean Kelly and Diran Apelian, Center for Resource Recovery and Recycling, Worcester Polytechnic Institute, 2009

11 *Industry Global Flows of Copper (2015) and Derived Recycling Rates,* World Copper Factbook 2017, International Copper Study Group

12 *Global Energy Statistical Yearbook 2019 – Energy*, Enerdata, 2019

13 *Coal consumption by sector in China 2008-2024*, International Energy Agency, 2019

14 *How China is improving coal technology*, Sonal Patel, Power, 6 June 2019

15 *Global Energy Statistical Yearbook 2019* – Coal, Enerdata, 2019

16 *Tesla just made its giant battery reserve in South Australia even bigger*, Susannah Guthrie, CarAdvice, 20 April 2020

17 *Creating the Twentieth Century: Technical innovations of 1867-1914 and Their Lasting Impact*, Vaclav Smil, Oxford University Press, 2005

18 *The Fourth Industrial Revolution*, Klaus Schwab, Penguin, 2014

19 *Hydrogen as a clean alternative in the iron and steel industry*, Quailann Homann, Fuel Cell and Hydrogen Energy Association, 2019

20 *Bauxite Mining in Africa*, Johannes Knierzinger, Palgrave MacMillan, 2018

21 *BHP quits Guinea after backdoor deal revealed*, Danny Fortson, The Times, 15 July 2012

22 *Why Robert Friedland is bullish on copper*, Valentina Leotaud, Mining. Com, 19 January 2018

23 *Copper Market Presentation: Copperbelt Research Trip*, May and June 2018, Hamish Sampson, CRU

24 *The giant Kamoa-Kakula Project in the Democratic Republic of the Congo*, S Amos, V Nkuna and B Matsetela, Journal of the South African Institute of Mining and Metallurgy, November 2018

25 *Estimate of Undiscovered Copper Resources of the World*, 2013, Kathleen M Johnson et al, United States Geological Survey, 2014

Made in the USA
Monee, IL
04 November 2026

67379643R00046